Organic | Vegan | Gluten Free | Natural Sweeteners

The Chakra Kitchen

Feed your Body to Nourish your Spirit

Sarah Wilkinson

To the earth, with gratitude for all
the bountiful produce gifted to us.

Published in 2015 by CICO Books
An imprint of Ryland Peters & Small Ltd

20–21 Jockey's Fields
London WC1R 4BW

341 E 116th St
New York, NY 10029

www.rylandpeters.com

10 9 8 7 6 5 4 3 2 1

ISBN: 978-1-78249-265-8

Printed in China

Editors: Gillian Haslam and Marion Paull
Designer: Niels van Gijn
Photographer: Adrian Lawrence
Stylist: Luis Peral
Home economist: Lizzie Harris

In-house editor: Dawn Bates
In-house designer: Fahema Khanam
Art director: Sally Powell
Production controller: Sarah Kulasek-Boyd
Publishing manager: Penny Craig
Publisher: Cindy Richards

Contents

Introduction

The Chakra Kitchen is the result of several years of working with chakra foods. Back in 2011, I began training in various healing modalities, attending workshops, and absorbing copious books. Soon, I decided to leave my 10-year career in the arts and higher education to pursue a spiritual path and to help others and the planet. My first business, Chakra Cakes, was born out of a light-hearted parting gift to my colleagues to introduce them to the ancient chakra system. Then came my signature Chakra Teas—Flame and Flora (formerly No. 1 and No. 2) —and savory catering at Mind, Body, Spirit events. Over the years, I have received some press and media attention and had the privilege of supplying cakes to Hay House publishers for their authors. This book is a beautiful and timely opportunity for me to share with you the benefits of eating foods to support your chakras and, in addition, how to harness the power of crystal energy in the preparation.

Conscious eating

This means taking a loving and caring interest in choosing, preparing, and eating your food. If you do this, you will automatically be working with your crown chakra, your spiritual gateway. Now there are many ways in which you can achieve a more conscious connection with food. One is to buy seasonal organic and biodynamic foods, local where possible (so lowering your carbon footprint). Another is to introduce veganism into your life, thereby respecting and extending love to all animal life as equal inhabitants of this planet. Meat and animal products have very dense vibrations—hence many people who are in touch with their spirituality increasingly turn to a vegan lifestyle to match their higher vibration. It is widely accepted that a diet high in meat consumption can cause excess fat, bad cholesterol, acidic blood, and a build-up of uric acid in the body, leading to joint problems.

As we rise in consciousness with the planet (which is happening rapidly now), our bodies are shifting. Food sensitivities and intolerances are an indication of this. Overprocessed foods containing modified wheat, such as supermarket bread, have high levels of gluten, and this is increasingly causing problems with digestion in a number of people. Avoiding gluten, or at least opting for freshly prepared food made with whole grains, such as spelt and rye, can help a sensitive system. Sugar consumption is something else to watch. As we all know by now, refined sugar, along with other stimulants, such as coffee, tea, and alcohol, are best taken in moderation, if at all. I have a sweet tooth, but have adjusted my diet over the past few years so that I use natural sweeteners, and on very rare occasions organic, unrefined sugar. I hope that the recipes in this book will help you to enjoy experimenting with sugar alternatives (see page 24).

We are all made of subtle vibrational energy and you can feel for the life force in a plant-based food by holding it in your hands and closing your eyes (once you get better at feeling energy, you won't need to close your eyes!), so take time to choose fruit and vegetables. When preparing meals, pour love into the ingredients. I once had a flatmate who automatically sang to her food as she chopped away in the kitchen. I used to laugh but now I understand why she was doing it—to connect, even if she wasn't conscious of that herself at the time. Once your meal is ready, serve it at the table and take a moment to thank the earth, the farmers, and producers as well as the food itself. Gratitude is always a winner! Try to share food with friends and family when possible and make it a sensual, joyous experience. Take the time to eat slowly, chewing and taking notice of the colors, textures, tastes, and aromas. You will digest with more ease, absorb more nutrients, and have an all-round beautiful experience. You will also feel fuller quicker. Overeating, or forcing yourself to consume anything you don't like, is not good. Learn to listen to your body. Food waste is best kept to a minimum for the sake of all and the planet, so try not to buy too much, and find creative ways to use up any spare ingredients, or donate to food banks.

Seasonal, organic and biodynamic foods

If you don't have an organic farm or market nearby, a good option is to order from an online box scheme, and many supermarkets stock a good range. Recent papers on the health benefits of organic foods over regular farmed crops indicate that higher concentrations of antioxidants and (poly)phenolics are present in the former. There are also lower concentrations of cadmium (toxic metal contaminant), nitrate, and chemical pesticide residues (*Organic versus Non-organic: A New Evaluation of Nutritional Difference/Crops*, Neal's Yard Remedies, July 2014). The beauty of biodynamic farming is that it not only works seasonally, but it also preserves and heals the land and increases harmony between man, plant, and animal. Those who eat biodynamic foods rave about the taste, aroma, and vibrancy of the crops. Pioneered by the teacher and philosopher Rudolf Steiner, the system makes use of the planetary associations with crops and the lunar calendar.

How to use this book

Each recipe has been color coded to the chakra system via a diagram at the top of the page. Please cross reference to the Chakra section of the book for in-depth information on what this means. The coding system highlights the chakras represented in the recipe, with those most predominant in bold. All recipes have the crown chakra highlighted as they contain organic foods and conscious intention in the preparation.

The Chakras

According to ancient Vedic texts (the Upanishads), there are seven major chakras on the body (and many more beyond). A chakra (meaning "wheel" in Sanskrit) is an energy center or vortex. Each one is represented by a color and quite often a lotus symbol. Chakras are portals through which we receive fresh energy to help us survive our incarnation, follow our true-life path, and grow in spirit. When a chakra is dysfunctional, that is underactive or overactive, problems can develop in the corresponding areas emotionally and/or psychically. It is extremely common for people to have imbalances in one or more of the chakras, and complete harmony throughout the system requires some effort. You can work with the chakras through exercise (yoga), meditation, complementary healing modalities, crystals, sound, and foods, thereby supporting general health and well-being.

Underactive chakras are caused by blocked or stagnant upward energy flow, which is held within the area. An example would be something untrue or "suppressive" that has been programed into a young child by a parent and remained imprinted within that child into adulthood. This would more often than not affect the functioning of the root chakra, since this is the first to develop and it acts as the foundation of the whole physical system. Stimulation of the chakra is required via any of the methods mentioned above, including the ingestion of certain foods.

Overactive chakras occur when too much energy is flowing through the area concerned, which can be due to underactive chakras on either side or from other external influences. A balance can be achieved by diverting energy to the chakras lying either side of that concerned, especially the higher one as energy tends to flow up and outwards from the body. Again, methods listed above can help, including the ingestion of balancing foods relating to this area, and potentially stimulating foods for the chakra that lies above that concerned.

Physical symptoms can be the same for either an underactive or overactive chakra. I recommend assessing emotional and behavioral characteristics to decide which is more likely for you. If in any doubt, please consult a chakra healer or therapist for guidance. In this book I am working specifically with foods and crystals, each of which have a particular effect on the chakras. Please see the Ingredients on pages 12–25 and Harnessing the Power of Crystals on pages 10–11 for further information and guidance for your specific needs.

The seven chakras

Colors are used to represent each of the seven chakras, the body's energy centers.

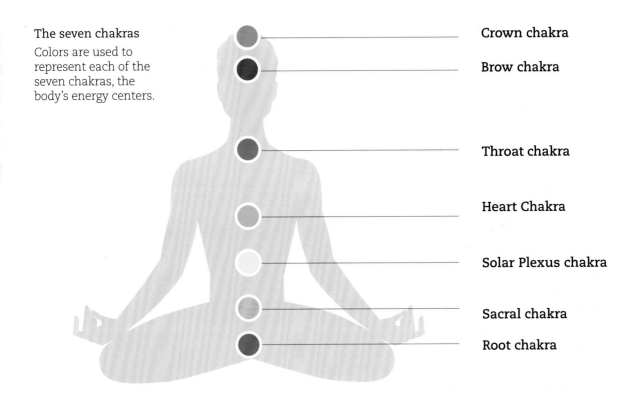

Crown chakra

Brow chakra

Throat chakra

Heart Chakra

Solar Plexus chakra

Sacral chakra

Root chakra

Root Chakra
(Mulhadara)

Location: Base of spine

Number: 1

Colors: Red, black, earthy tones

Symbol: Lotus with four petals

Gender: Masculine

Element: Earth

Function: Security, survival, physical well-being, family, grounding, tribe, tradition

Signs of underactivity: Spaced out and a bit lost in the world, disconnected and flighty, self-centered, disorganized, lack of stamina, financial insecurities, fear, co-dependency.

Signs of overactivity: Stuck in the mud, uneasy with change and the natural flow of life, anger toward situations and people, overmaterialistic, greedy and controlling, not in touch with your spiritual essence, impatient.

Physical signs of dysfunction: Poor immune system, skeletal issues, bone marrow disease, lower-back problems, leg and foot pains, depression, fatigue, low sex drive, circulatory problems, constipation, rectum problems and weight issues.

Signs of function: You flow with the world and it flows with you; you have few problems with relationships, finance, or work; you are comfortable in your own skin and have good overall physical health.

Affirmation: "I am one with the earth, secure in the knowledge that I am valued, well provided for, and nourished at all times."

Sacral chakra
(Svadisthana)

Location: Just below the navel area

Number: 2

Colors: Orange, amber

Symbol: Lotus with six petals

Gender: Feminine

Element: Water

Function: Emotions, sexuality, pleasure, joy, creativity

Signs of underactivity: Fear of pleasure, self-denial, making excuses not to go for what you want, lack of creative flow, no sense of your own identity, always trying to fit in with what you perceive to be "the norm," detachment.

Signs of overactivity: Overemotional, tendency to be a drama queen, unhealthy attachments to people leading to upset if they "let you down," mania, anxiety.

Physical signs of dysfunction: Tense muscles, laziness, pains in lower abdomen, lower back pain, urinary and kidney infections, constipation, diarrhoea, overly high or low sex drive, gynecological and menstrual problems, testicular or prostate disease.

Signs of Function: You can speak and show your feelings freely and without reserve; you have self-confidence and balanced sexuality meaning that intimacy comes as no problem and you are able to cope with anything life throws at you, moving forward with a lust for life.

Affirmation:"I feel my way forward on my soul journey, creating, pleasuring, and flowing with joy as I go."

Solar Plexus chakra
(Manipura)

Location: Just below the sternum and above the navel

Number: 3

Colors: Yellow, gold

Symbol: Lotus with ten petals

Element: Fire

Gender: Masculine

Function: Seat of power, willpower, self-perception, transformation

Signs of underactivity: Emotional imbalance, feeling not good enough, worrying about another's opinion of you, avoiding your true feelings, seeking constant approval from others, unable to assert authority or individuality in the workplace, inability to save or attain money.

Signs of overactivity: Feelings of anger, aggressiveness, having fixed opinions, being stubborn, workaholic, perfectionist, ego driven.

Physical signs of dysfunction: Ulcers, diabetes, digestive and eating disorders, fluctuating weight, liver and kidney problems.

Signs of function: You radiate warmth and joy toward yourself and others, have well-balanced emotions, control of the ego, along with respect for yourself and others.

Affirmation: "I burn brightly, centered in my power and truth, sharing my passions with the world. I can, I am, and I do."

Heart Chakra
(Anahata)

Location: Center of your chest

Number: 4

Colors: Green, rose pink

Symbol: Lotus with 12 petals

Gender: Female

Element: Air

Function: Center of unconditional love, gratitude, joy, empathy, loyalty, forgiveness

Signs of underactivity: Feelings of being unloved and unappreciated, lack of emotion, difficulty trusting, hard to let people get close to you, binge eating as a result of lack of self-love (can also relate to a sacral-chakra imbalance linked to emotions).

Signs of overactivity: Conditional rather than unconditional loving, co-dependency, being manipulative, controlling, emotions control you.

Physical signs of dysfunction: Palpitations, heart attacks, circulatory problems, high or low blood pressure and stress.

Signs of function: You feel at ease with people, have great compassion for all living creatures, are comfortable in your own company, exuding love and enjoyment.

Affirmation: "I am love. I radiate love for myself, for all other living organisms, and for planet Earth."

Throat Chakra
(Visuddha)

Location: Throat

Number: 5

Colors: Sky blue, turquoise, aqua, silver

Symbol: Lotus with 16 petals

Gender: Masculine

Element: Ether

Function: Center of expression, communication, speaking your truth, self-knowledge, authenticity, taste, hearing.

Signs of underactivity: Inability to communicate, express creativity, feelings and emotions; procrastination, stagnation, flakiness and difficulty in being honest.

Signs of overactivity: Speaking before you think, overopinionated, regularly raising your voice to interrupt others, not accepting what others say.

Physical signs of dysfunction: Sore throat, tonsillitis, laryngitis, ear problems, jaw problems, neck pains, shoulder and/or arm aches, swollen lymph glands, toothache

Signs of function: You have the ability to communicate effectively, with no fear of expressing yourself or showing your weaknesses and a willingness to offer positive advice when asked, clear and creative self-expression.

Affirmation: "I am able both to listen and speak with ease and grace. I express my true feelings as they arise with control and balance."

Brow Chakra
(Ajna)

Location: Above and in between the eyes

Number: 6

Colors: Dark blue, indigo

Symbol: Lotus with two petals

Element: Light

Gender: Feminine

Function: Center of intuition and psychic awareness, inner wisdom, imagination, cognition, perception, mood, sleep, dreams.

Signs of underactivity: Disconnection from your spiritual essence, problems with memory, lack of common sense and empathy.

Signs of overactivity: Tension in head, overly intellectual, delusional, regular nightmares.

Physical signs of dysfunction: Headaches around the temples, migraines, insomnia, dizziness, brain tumors, sinus problems and hormonal imbalance.

Signs of function: You have reliable intuition, and the ability to connect with your higher self and receive messages from angels and spiritual guides, with no problems absorbing and remembering new information.

Affirmation: "I follow my intuition in all that I do and trust that it is always for my highest good."

Crown Chakra
(Sahasrara)

Location: Top of head

Number: 7

Colors: Violet, white, transparent

Symbol: Lotus with 1,000 petals

Gender: Genderless

Element: Consciousness

Function: Spirituality, unity, all that is, infinity, bliss, higher self awareness, awakening, eternity.

Signs of underactivity: Feelings of being unloved and having no life purpose, general lack of positivity, difficulty in understanding the greater picture and the concept of your universal/higher self, lack of spirituality, anger toward God, fear of death.

Signs of overactivity: Spaced out, difficulty in relating to the world around you, having spontaneous out-of-body experiences and frequent encounters with other realms of existence, considering yourself superior to others.

Physical signs of dysfunction: Exhaustion, Chronic Fatigue Syndrome, muscular and skin disorders, sensitivity to light and sound.

Signs of function: You have wisdom, compassion, and reliable intuition; understanding all that is and the connection of every living thing, your place on earth and the role you play and willingness to help others.

Affirmation: "I am one with nature, the universe, and all that is. I have infinite, higher wisdom."

HARNESSING THE POWER OF CRYSTALS

In preparing food, the healing powers of the ingredients used can be boosted by the presence of crystals. Here are some guidelines and examples of crystals to use when working with each chakra.

- Begin with a suitable Root-chakra crystal (see below) and, if non-porous, hold it under running water for a few minutes or pass it through incense smoke a few times. I tend to use the latter option. As you do this, focus on any impurities and stagnant or unwanted energies flowing out from the crystal.

- Now hold the crystal over your Heart chakra and imagine white light radiating into the stone directly from you. This will empower the crystal with your energy. Effectively, you are charging it up.

- When you intuitively sense that the crystal is filled with enough energy, dedicate it to empowering Root-chakra foods by either silently asking or speaking out loud something along the lines of "[crystal name] please provide the right amount of healing energy to support the root-chakra foods I'm using in my recipes."

- Repeat this process with the remaining chakra crystals and adjust your words accordingly for each dedication.

Amethyst

If you wish to use the crystals for laying-on healing in addition to preparing the recipes, simply add a few words to this effect when you are dedicating the crystals, so that they are charged for the dual purpose.

Red Jasper

CRYSTAL	CHAKRA	FUNCTION
Black Tourmaline	Root	Protects against negative energy; grounds and provides a sense of security; powerful healer of mental disorders; strengthens the will to meet change and new challenges; aids detox and supports healthy weight loss.
Hematite	Root	Grounds, anchors, and supports all aspects of mind and body; good to have around when feeling spaced out; can help you to realize spiritual concepts and dreams; tonic for the blood and circulatory system.
Red Jasper	Root	Grounds, spiritually and emotionally; tonic for the whole body, powerful healer, able to soothe emotions; helps create a focused environment in meditation; brings clarity and new ideas, eases change; brings problems to a head to be dealt with before they grow too big; can reduce digestive disorders; supports stamina by encouraging slow release of energy.
Orange Calcite	Sacral	Balances emotions along with masculine and feminine energies; grounds excessive enthusiasm and inspires joy and happiness; supports kidneys and lower digestive function (can help to ease IBS).
Carnelian	Sacral	Helps to heal gallbladder, kidneys, and pancreas; aids tissue regeneration; good balancer and energizer, reinforcing connection with the inner self; boosts creativity, sexuality, self-esteem; helps to balance masculine and feminine energies; friendly and healing.

Crocoite	Sacral	Stimulates sexual activity, tantra, and passion; provides stamina in life-changing situations; promotes new ideas; brings confidence in the self, especially in relationships; boosts creativity.
Amber	Solar Plexus	Good for supporting the spleen and endocrine system; promotes success and achievement, clearing the mind and easing stress; transformational, bringing luck and purification.
Citrine	Solar Plexus	Protects and brings self-empowerment; attracts wealth; very good for healing the gallbladder, digestive organs, and kidneys; prevents self-destructive tendencies, helping to raise self-esteem; known as the "sunshine stone," light-hearted and warming.
Tiger's Eye	Solar Plexus	Uplifting, encourages a sense of self-worth and self-confidence; adds positivity and optimism for achieving life goals, stepping into power, and recognizing talents; releases blocked creativity and encourages wealth and prosperity.
Bloodstone	Heart	Enhances mental and physical well-being and detoxes the body; brings inspiration and supports intuition; boosts courage and self-esteem.
Jade	Heart	Strengthens the heart with its subtle vibration, and cleans the blood; balances emotions, and can ease female problems; oozes with unconditional Divine love, and nurtures, providing clarity and wisdom; focuses mind and heart on achieving dreams.
Rose Quartz	Heart	The love stone, helps the heart to open; provides a sense of self-worth and comfort; supports relationships; helps to release guilt and anger, and said to help keep youthful looks and boost fertility.
Amazonite	Heart/Throat	Resonates with both the heart and throat chakras; aids communication, confidence, and speaking your truth through boosting self-expression; good to carry when speaking in public or dealing with a difficult situation.
Apatite	Throat	Helps with personal expression and communication, encouraging a flexible attitude; activates the intellect and deepens understanding; helps with teeth and bone health.
Turquoise	Throat	Enhances communication (including with Spirit), creative expression, and peace of mind; provides safety by strengthening and enhancing the aura; eases many ailments, helping all organs; promotes friendship and romance through balancing the heart and thymus along with the throat.
Azurite	Brow	Stimulates creativity; assists with expressing deep thoughts and emotions; connects you with the Divine for guidance; improves clairvoyance; helps with decision making, cuts through illusion.
Lapis Lazuli	Brow	For vitality and also relaxation; promotes clarity and connection with the higher self, strengthening intuition and psychic abilities and inspiring creative expression; helps with organization; mood enhancer.
Sodalite	Brow	Calms and clears the mind; alleviates fear and brings clarity and truth; enhances communication and insight by strengthening metabolism; benefits communication with the higher self.
Amethyst	Crown	Strengthens the immune system; improves right-brain activity, pineal, and pituitary glands; blood cleanser and energizer; enhances spiritual development; cuts through illusion, inspiring healing and intuition.
Clear Quartz	Crown	A must! Balances all chakras and brings immense healing via the crown; attracts optimism, light, and joy, so aids meditation and releases negative blocks; amplifies the energies of other crystals around it and can re-energize during sleep if placed by the bedside.
Selenite	Crown	Rejuvenates the body; helps to keep the skin youthful and prevent hair loss; boosts longevity; encourages a positive flow in life, through its lunar energies, unblocking the crown chakra and shifting negative emotions, darkness, and stagnant energy.

Amber

Rose Quartz

Lapis Lazuli

INGREDIENTS

These days, many fruits and vegetables are available all through the year but, where possible, I prefer to eat seasonally, and organically grown, to get the best flavors, aromas, and textures. They are full of amazing nutrients and, especially important, antioxidants. These are necessary to protect the body from free radicals, which cause chronic disease, including heart disease and cancer. Vitamins C and E and betacarotene (which the body converts into vitamin A) are powerful antioxidants, as are flavonoids and polyphenols (also referred to as phytonutrients and phytochemicals). In addition, vitamin C fights viral infection, vitamin E is especially beneficial for the skin and eyes and may help relieve arthritic pain, and both boost the immune system. Betacarotene (vitamin A) is good for the eyes and protects the lungs. Vitamin K is good for bone health and blood clotting, and helps to prevent heart disease, while the B vitamins are energy boosting and good for the brain. One essential vitamin that lacks in a vegan diet is B12, so supplementation is generally advised.

Vitamins and minerals generally support the cardiovascular system. Among essential minerals, potassium helps the heart to function well, potentially lowers blood pressure, and supports fluid levels in the body. Manganese supports strong bones and connective tissue. Calcium builds strong bones and teeth, regulates heartbeat and other muscle contractions, and ensures normal blood clotting. Magnesium is necessary for bone health, and the proper functioning of nerves and muscles. It also aids digestion, helps the body to form protein, and supports energy levels. Foods high in fiber generally contain magnesium. Dietary fiber is important—soluble fiber aids digestion, may affect blood-sugar levels, and can help lower LDL (bad) cholesterol; insoluble fiber helps to relieve constipation.

Omega-3 and Omega-6 fatty acids, found in kale, and some nuts and seeds, are anti-inflammatory. They support heart and brain function, and help to reduce LDL cholesterol and maintain healthy blood-pressure levels.

When it comes to plant-based milks, I tend to purchase organic, unsweetened varieties (rather than make my own) for ease and cost such as almond, brown rice, hemp, oat (gluten free), and soya.

Oils all support the duality of the sacral chakra and vinegars stimulate the Solar Plexus and Brow chakras. On the whole, unsaturated fats are the healthiest and the following are a good source (and also support the Heart chakra): canola (rapeseed) oil, extra virgin olive oil, sesame oil, sunflower oil. I also use coconut oil, which contains saturated fat (see page 21).

Whenever possible, I use purified or mineral water. Water balances the Sacral, Throat, and Crown chakras. All ingredients in these recipes support at least one chakra, and usually several, and are available in wholefood stores and many supermarkets.

FRUIT	ASSOCIATED CHAKRAS & PURPOSE	EFFECT	NUTRITIONAL CONTENT AND BENEFITS
Apples	Root, Solar Plexus	B	Soluble fiber, vitamin C, and polyphenols; fat free.
Apricots (soft dried)	Sacral	S	Vitamins A, B3, C, K, and E; high in potassium and insoluble fiber.
Avocados	Root, Sacral, Heart	B	Good levels of vitamins B5 and E; vitamin E coupled with high levels of oleic acid (or omega-9, a monounsaturated fat) limits risk of heart attack/strokes and reduces LDL cholesterol; immune-boosting, anti-inflammatory, blood-sugar-regulating.
Bananas	Solar Plexus, Brow	S	High in potassium; magnesium and tryptophan (amino acid) help with stress reduction and aid sleep; vitamin A; energy-boosting.
Blackberries	Brow	B	High in vitamins C and K; color comes from anthocyanins (antioxidants), which support overall health.
Blueberries	Heart, Brow	B	Good levels of fiber, manganese, and vitamins C and K; help to prevent degenerative eye disease; support cardiovascular health via anthocyanidins (antioxidant compounds).
Cranberries	Root, Sacral, Heart	S	Best known for urinary tract support due to proanthocyanidins, which prevent e. coli bacteria from attaching to the urethra wall; also contain phytonutrients and are beneficial to heart health.
Cucumber	Heart, Throat	B	Antioxidant and anti-inflammatory cucurbitacins, lignans, and flavonoids; high water content.
Dates	Sacral, Solar Plexus	S	Various vitamins, minerals, natural sugars, and soluble fiber; can help with weight gain and be useful in boosting sexual stamina.
Figs (soft dried)	Sacral, Solar Plexus	S	Good levels of potassium and calcium; high in soluble fiber.
Goji berries	Root, Brow	S	See page 25.
Grapes (black)	Solar Plexus, Throat, Brow	B	Contains anthocyanins (antioxidants), which support overall health.
Kiwis	Sacral, Heart, Throat	S	High in nutrients, low in calories; rich in vitamin C and potassium; soluble fiber.
Lemons	Root, Solar Plexus, Throat	S	Excellent source of vitamin C; alkalizing and, combined with hot water, good to kick start digestion.
Limes	Root, Heart, Throat	S	Flavonoids and acids that aid digestion; soluble fiber; similar nutritional components to lemons.
Mandarins/oranges	Sacral, Brow	S	Dietary fiber; vitamin C; betacarotene.
Mango	Sacral, Throat	B	Full of betacarotene and active enzymes that help to break down protein; best eaten before a meal or alone to aid digestion.
Olives (black)	Root, Sacral, Heart, Brow	B	Rich source of soluble fiber; high levels of monounsaturated fats, which (in moderation) can support heart health.

B = Balance | S = Stimulate

FRUIT	ASSOCIATED CHAKRAS & PURPOSE	EFFECT	NUTRITIONAL CONTENT AND BENEFITS
Papaya	Sacral, Solar Plexus, Brow	B	Contains the enzyme papain, which helps to break down protein; vitamins C, E, B9 (folate), and betacarotene, which help to reduce inflammation and promote good colon and eye health.
Passion fruit	Sacral, Brow	B	High in potassium; good source of vitamins A and C; contains alkaloids that can help alleviate insomnia and anxiety.
Pears	Heart	B	Soluble fiber (half of it in the skin); flavonoids; can help to reduce the risk of inflammatory heart disease and type 2 diabetes.
Pineapples	Root, Sacral, Solar Plexus, Throat	B	High levels of vitamins C and B1, and manganese; enzyme bromelain, which helps to break down proteins; low in sodium and fat; cholesterol free.
Plums	Root, Solar Plexus, Throat, Brow	B	Rich in potassium, fluoride, and iron; moderate source of B vitamins; high in anti-inflammatory antioxidants.
Pumpkins	Root, Sacral, Solar Plexus, Heart, Brow	B	High levels of potassium, betacarotene, fiber, and vitamin C.
Raisins	Sacral, Solar Plexus, Brow	S	Energy-boosting fructose and glucose; dietary fiber; arginine, amino acid that boosts libido; phytonutrients; betacarotene.
Raspberries	Root, Brow	S	Rich in vitamin C and manganese; reasonable levels of vitamins K and E and lower levels of other vitamins and minerals; flavonoids that can help with memory improvement and cognitive ability during the aging process; can also help with suppressing inflammation.
Squash (winter)	Root, Sacral, Solar Plexus, Heart, Brow	B	Packed with betacarotene and good levels of vitamin C and potassium; similar properties to pumpkins.
Strawberries	Root, Heart	S	High in vitamin C and manganese; antioxidant and anti-inflammatory nutrients that support the cardiovascular system; studies have shown a reduced risk of type 2 diabetes from regular consumption; can help with wound healing.
Tomatoes	Root, Heart, Throat	S	Contains lycopene (phytochemical); vitamins C, E, and betacarotene.
Zucchini (courgette)	Solar Plexus, Heart, Throat	B	Good levels of vitamin C and potassium; soluble fiber in the skin.

B = Balance | S = Stimulate

VEGETABLES	ASSOCIATED CHAKRAS & PURPOSE	EFFECT	NUTRITIONAL CONTENT AND BENEFITS
Arugula (rocket)	Heart	B	Good levels of vitamins C and K; in traditional Arabic medicine, believed to be an aphrodisiac—research ongoing.
Asparagus	Sacral, Heart	S	High in vitamin K; mildly anti-inflammatory; increases urinary output via the compound asparagine, so can be useful in cases of fluid retention and high blood pressure.
Beet (beetroot)	Root, Heart	B	High in nitrates, which help to reduce blood pressure; particularly beneficial as juice; improves muscle oxygenation.
Broccoli	Heart	B	High in vitamins K and C; anti-inflammatory and lessens the impact of allergy-related substances; steamed broccoli can help to lower LDL cholesterol.
Brussels sprouts	Heart	B	High in glucosinolates, which the body converts into cancer-fighting substances; good source of vitamins C and K, manganese, and flavonoids.
Carrots	Root, Sacral, Solar Plexus, Heart, Brow	B	High in betacarotene, beneficial to eye and skin health. Low in calories and lower the risk of cardiovascular disease.
Celery	Sacral, Heart, Throat	B	High in water content, low in calories; diuretic, due to potassium and coumarin levels, which can help relieve urinary tract infections and lower blood pressure; good levels of vitamins A, K, and E; natural pain reliever and known allergen.
Celery root (celeriac)	Root, Sacral	B	High in antioxidants and vitamin K; diuretic and an allergen.
Chard (rainbow)	Heart	B	Good source of vitamin K, iron, magnesium, manganese, and copper; stems are high in phytochemicals that can help to reduce risk of heart disease and diabetes; avoid if prone to kidney stones (contains oxalates that can reduce calcium absorption and potentially lead to formation of stones).
Collard (spring greens)	Heart	B	High in vitamins C and K; anti-inflammatory phytochemicals that could help to protect against heart disease and stroke; enzymes that support detox.
Eggplants (aubergine)	Solar Plexus, Brow	B	High in dietary fiber; good source of vitamins B1 and B6 and potassium; phytonutrient nasunin, which may protect brain cell membranes.
Garlic	Root, Solar Plexus, Heart	S	Antiviral, anti-inflammatory (raw), and protects against blood clotting; excessive consumption not recommended if on drugs to lower blood pressure.
Jerusalem artichokes	Root, Solar Plexus	B	Prebiotic inulin (a form of carbohydrate dietary fiber that feeds probiotic organisms, which in turn can boost immune function and prevent "bad" bacteria from increasing); phosphorus, which can help to strengthen bones and DNA.
Kale	Root, Heart	B	Rich in vitamins A, C, and K; high in calcium and phosphorus for bone health, and chlorophyll for muscle ease; omega-3 fatty acids and phytochemicals provide support to the cardiovascular system.

VEGETABLES	ASSOCIATED CHAKRAS & PURPOSE	EFFECT	NUTRITIONAL CONTENT AND BENEFITS
Leeks	Root, Heart	S, B	Good source of vitamin B6, which reduces the risk of blood clotting, and the flavonoid kaempferol, which protects blood vessel linings; contains the prebiotic inulin that aids colon health and immunity.
Lettuce	Heart	B	Antioxidants for overall good health; can help to lower LDL cholesterol; low in calories.
Mushrooms	Root, Brow	B	Only vegan food source of vitamin D (necessary for the absorption of calcium); rich in B vitamins and choline, which can aid sleep, learning, and memory; Shiitake mushrooms contain polysaccharides, which increase production of white blood cells and so support immune system.
Onions (red), shallots scallions (spring onions)	Root, Solar Plexus, Throat	S	Contains the prebiotic inulin, which supports digestive health phytochemicals that work with vitamin C; a compound that is thought to balance blood-sugar levels (but should not be used as a substitute for insulin); antibacterial, anti-inflammatory, antifungal; have been used in folk medicine to relieve coughs, colds, and catarrh.
Parsnips	Root, Solar Plexus	B	High in dietary fiber, and nutrients including potassium, folate (B9), and vitamin C. ; Also contains inulin to support digestive health.
Pepper (green bell) **Pepper (red bell)**	Heart, Solar Plexus, Throat Root, Solar Plexus, Throat	B B	High in a variety of carotenoids (antioxidant plant pigments); the red variety hold the most nutrition as they have ripened on the vine for longest and contain more vitamin C and betacarotene than other colors.
Potatoes	Root, Solar Plexus	S	Good levels of vitamins C and B6.
Rhubarb	Root, Heart	B	Reasonable source of calcium and carotenoid lutein, which is good for the eyes; leaves should be avoided due to high levels of oxalic acid.
Rutabaga (swede)	Root, Solar Plexus	B	Good source of vitamins C and B6, betacarotene, potassium, manganese, calcium, and fiber; antioxidant and antifungal; low in calories.
Spinach	Root, Sacral, Heart	B	Good source of vitamins A, C, K, and folate; high in carotenoids.
Sweet potatoes	Root, Sacral, Solar Plexus	B	Rich in betacarotene; good source of fiber; fat free and low GI, containing slow-release sugars, which helps with controlling blood-sugar levels and maintaining energy.
Watercress	Heart	B	Full of natural phytonutrients, low in calories, rich in vitamins A, B, C, and K; a good source of minerals, including potassium and calcium to support cardiovascular and bone health.

B = Balance | S = Stimulate

LEGUMES

Legumes have a high protein content and so tend to form a substantial part of a vegan diet. They are natural diuretics, supporting the sacral chakra, and act as carbohydrates, affecting the Solar Plexus chakra. Legumes fill you up without adding much to your calorie consumption (low-energy-dense foods). Beans contain good amounts of the mineral molybdenum, which can support enzymes that synthesize amino acids and help with the removal of toxins from the liver. Due to legumes' high fiber content, across the board they support the cardiovascular system (Heart chakra) by removing excess cholesterol. Sprouting legumes are highly recommended for consumption during the spring. Sprouts are packed full of nutrients and so easy to cultivate at home. All you need are a couple of sprouting jars or a sprouter, which are widely available. I also like to grow larger shoots, such as snow peas, which requires a slightly different process (see page 35).

LEGUMES	ASSOCIATED CHAKRAS & PURPOSE	EFFECTS	NUTRITIONAL CONTENT AND BENEFITS
Adzuki (aduki) beans	Root, Sacral, Solar Plexus, Heart	B	Rich in carbohydrates, protein, fiber, and folic acid; reasonable levels of iron and potassium.
Black turtle beans	Root, Sacral, Solar Plexus, Heart	B	High in molybdenum; supports lower digestive tract.
Butter beans	Root, Sacral, Solar Plexus, Heart	B	Good source of B vitamins, as well as zinc (for immune support) and magnesium.
Chickpeas	Root, Sacral, Solar Plexus, Heart	B	Good levels of immune-boosting and skin-healing zinc, and fiber; isoflavone compounds act in a similar way to oestrogen; antioxidant.
Fava (broad) beans	Root, Sacral, Solar Plexus, Heart	B	Rich in folate (B9) and other B vitamins; good for energy levels and blood-cell development; high in potassium; one of the few natural sources of Levodopa (L-dopa), which is used in the treatment of Parkinson's disease; best eaten fresh.
Fine green beans	Root, Sacral, Solar Plexus, Heart	B	Good source of antioxidants, fiber, and carotene; good levels of silicon, which is useful for bones and the healthy formation of connective tissue.
Kidney beans	Root, Sacral, Solar Plexus, Heart	B	Rich in folate (B9), magnesium, and fiber; support the cardiovascular system.
Lentils	Root, Sacral, Solar Plexus, Heart	B	Full of B vitamins and magnesium.
Mung beans	Root, Sacral, Solar Plexus, Heart	B	Rich in magnesium, potassium, vitamins B6 and folate (B9); easier to digest than black beans, when sprouted, provide higher levels of vitamins C and K; used in Chinese medicine to reduce toxicity and cleanse the vascular system.
Peas/petit pois	Sacral, Heart	B	Good source of folate (B9) and vitamin K; pea shoots high in vitamin C and essential amino acids needed to make protein.
Soy/tofu	Root, Sacral, Solar Plexus, Heart	B	Made from soy beans, tofu is cholesterol-free protein and a natural source of iron and calcium, supporting bone and cell health; provides the full spectrum of essential amino acids and contains isoflavones, which can support female reproductive health.

SEAWEED AND MICRO-ALGAE

Sea plants are a fantastic source of chlorophyll, iodine, and other nutrients. Taken as supplements or eaten as side dishes, they have a balancing effect, predominantly on the throat chakra.

SEAWEEDS & MICRO-ALGAE	ASSOCIATED CHAKRAS & PURPOSE	EFFECTS	NUTRITIONAL CONTENT AND BENEFITS
Agar (agar-agar)	Root, Heart, Throat	B	Composed of the mucilage (glutinous carbohydrate) of several species of seaweeds; good source of calcium and iron; often used as a vegan replacement for gelatine; low in calories; have a mild laxative effect; can aid with weight loss; helps to carry toxins from the body and reduce inflammation.
Chlorella	Root, Sacral, Heart, Throat	B	Rich nutrient content; superfood micro-algae; boosts energy, improves digestion, promotes healthy intestinal flora; carries heavy metals and pesticides out of the body; high levels of chlorophyll and nucleic acid strengthen immune system and reduce inflammation; high levels of fatty acids help reduce LDL cholesterol and prevent heart disease.
Kelp	Root, Sacral, Heart, Throat	B	Micro-algae rich in iodine (regulates thyroid and pituitary function); good levels of iron, calcium, and potassium; used as salt substitute due to high mineral content; natural diuretic; helps to strengthen nails and support hair growth; can eradicate fungal and candida yeast overgrowths; relieves respiratory tract problems, such as coughs and asthma; can help to moderate blood pressure and clotting; often used to aid weight loss.
Nori	Root, Heart, Throat	B	Rich in vitamins A and B, iron and magnesium; moderate levels of calcium; highest protein content of any seaweed and most easily digested; can help to lower LDL cholesterol and blood pressure.

B = Balance | **S** = Stimulate

HERBS AND SPICES

Generally speaking, herbs and spices are stimulating, and work mainly through the Brow, Root, and Sacral chakras. They all have vast nutritional and healing properties and have long been used in ayurvedic medicine. In vegan cuisine, their flavors and aromas can really "make" a dish.

HERBS & SPICES	ASSOCIATED CHAKRAS & PURPOSE	EFFECTS	NUTRITIONAL CONTENT AND BENEFITS
Aloe vera	Sacral, Solar Plexus, Heart, Throat	B	Mildly laxative and anti-inflammatory; often used to treat sunburn and to ease sore throats; helps to reduce LDL cholesterol and increase HDL (good) cholesterol.
Anise (star)	Root, Sacral, Brow	S	Antifungal (anti-candida) and antibacterial; improves immune system when combined with the flavonoid quercetin.
Basil	Sacral, Heart, Throat, Brow	S	Relieves catarrh and sinus inflammation (with steam bath); when ingested, helps inflammatory intestinal conditions; possible aphrodisiac.
Black pepper	Root, Sacral, Heart, Brow	S	Can boost appetite, stimulate digestion, help relieve constipation, and prevent flatulence.
Burdock root	Root, Sacral, Heart, Brow	S	Diuretic; blood cleanser; contains insulin, which regulates blood-sugar levels.
Caraway	Sacral, Solar Plexus, Throat, Brow	S	Good source of B vitamins and antioxidants; overall tonic, helping digestion and to prevent flatulence; expectorant, alleviating respiratory tract problems and laryngitis.
Cardamom	Root, Sacral, Solar Plexus, Brow	S	Good for digestion and preventing flatulence; may boost energy, stimulate sex drive, and help with relieving impotence.
Cayenne	Root, Solar Plexus, Heart, Throat, Brow	S	Anti-irritant; can relieve coughs and digestive upsets; breaks up mucus in the body, easing colds; can help to prevent atherosclerosis and blood clotting; best avoided when stomach ulcers or gastritis are present.
Celery seeds	Root, Sacral, Brow	S	Good source of calcium; diuretic.
Chili	Root, Heart, Brow	S	Good source of capsaicin, a phytochemical that helps to reduce blood pressure and boost circulation; natural pain reliever; helps in release of endorphins (feel-good hormones).
Cinnamon	Sacral, Solar Plexus, Brow	S	Disinfectant and can ease diarrhea; helps control blood-sugar levels and metabolism.
Clover (red)	Solar Plexus, Heart, Brow	B	Calming; aids digestion; excellent blood purifier; helps to remove toxins.
Cloves	Root, Sacral, Solar Plexus, Throat, Brow	S	Stimulant, expectorant, disinfectant, and prevents flatulence; commonly used to relieve toothache and to freshen the breath; in ayurvedic medicine, used to relieve chest infections and colds; also used to aid sexual function.
Coriander	Solar Plexus, Throat Brow	S	Helps to lower LDL and raise HDL (good) cholesterol levels; helps to lower blood pressure, aids digestion, and prevents flatulence.
Cumin	Root, Sacral, Solar Plexus, Brow	S	Good source of vitamin C; antiviral and brings relief for colds; aids digestion, prevents flatulence; expectorant.

HERBS & SPICES	ASSOCIATED CHAKRAS & PURPOSE	EFFECTS	NUTRITIONAL CONTENT AND BENEFITS
Dandelion root	Root, Sacral, Solar Plexus, Brow	S	Diuretic, which helps expel rheumatism acids; general tonic; aids digestion.
Ginger	Root, Solar Plexus, Brow	S	Antiseptic, antispasmodic, anti-inflammatory; relieves colds and chills; alleviates nausea; prevents flatulence.
Mint	Solar Plexus, Heart, Throat, Brow	S	Antioxidant and antiseptic; aids digestion and prevents flatulence; alleviates nausea; freshens the breath.
Nettle	Root, Sacral, Solar Plexus, Heart, Brow	S	Immune-boosting and diuretic; general tonic; astringent, hemostatic, gets rid of intestinal worms, and can lower blood sugar.
Nigella seeds (black cumin)	Root, Sacral, Throat, Brow	S	Antioxidant, anti-inflammatory, anti-allergenic; can be used in anti-candida diets and in helping to relieve upper respiratory infections and in the prevention of auto-immunodeficiency disorders.
Nutmeg	Root, Sacral, Solar Plexus, Brow	S	Helps prevent vomiting and soothes the nervous system; in small amounts acts as a sedative, for instance with warm milk; dangerous in large amounts (can have similar effects to hallucinogenic drugs and amphetamines).
Paprika	Root, Brow	S	Rich in vitamin A and carotenoids.
Parsley	Root, Sacral, Heart, Brow	S	High in vitamin C; good for urine flow by stimulating the kidneys; freshens the breath if chewed.
Rose	Heart	B	Rich in polyphenols and other antioxidants, which can help to prevent cardiovascular disease.
Rosemary	Heart, Brow	S	Diuretic, antispasmodic, antiseptic, vasodilatory, anti-inflammatory; general tonic; eases headaches and helps concentration; traditionally, brings peaceful sleep.
Saffron	Sacral, Brow	S	Good source of vitamins A, C, some Bs, minerals, and many carotenoids; antispasmodic; prevents flatulence; induces menstrual blood flow.
Sumac	Root, Solar Plexus, Heart, Brow	B	Potential antifungal and antioxidant properties; may help regulate blood sugar and promote cardiovascular health.
Tarragon	Sacral, Solar Plexus, Heart, Brow	S	Relieves bloating and helps to boost appetite; has been used to aid with suppressed menstrual flow and female reproductive health (not during pregnancy); antioxidant; supports the cardiovascular system.
Thyme	Root, Sacral, Solar Plexus, Heart, Brow	S	Antibiotic, antioxidant, antispasmodic, antibacterial; prevents flatulence; expectorant; helps alleviate respiratory tract conditions and gastrointestinal disorders, such as diarrhea.
Turmeric	Root, Sacral, Solar Plexus, Heart, Brow	S	Supports the liver, and digestive and cardiovascular systems; anti-inflammatory.
Vanilla bean	Solar Plexus, Brow	S	Complex sugars, essential oils, and some reasonable levels of B vitamins, which can help with cognitive function; trace amounts of minerals.

B = Balance | S = Stimulate

NUTS

If you can tolerate them, nuts are a great source of essential fatty acids and protein in vegan cuisine. In some of the recipes containing nuts I have suggested an alternative, or omission where possible, for allergy sufferers. I do not use peanuts at all (in fact, peanuts are legumes). For almonds, cashews, hazelnuts, pecans, and walnuts, I would recommend soaking them overnight before dehydrating. This neutralizes the enzyme inhibitors present in these nuts, which prevent nutrients from being absorbed by the body. You can purchase commercial dehydrators, or spread the nuts out on a baking tray and place in an oven at the lowest temperature overnight. All nuts balance the root and sacral chakras due to their grounding protein and healthy fats. The majority are helpful in supporting cardiovascular health and blood-sugar regulation, fostering the Solar Plexus and Heart chakras.

NUTS	ASSOCIATED CHAKRAS & PURPOSE	EFFECTS	NUTRITIONAL CONTENT AND BENEFITS
Almonds	Root, Sacral, Solar Plexus, Heart	B	Good levels of calcium and omega-6.
Brazils	Root, Sacral, Heart, Throat	B	High in vitamin E and selenium, which together provide immune-boosting properties; selenium can help to prevent heart disease and candida, and to relieve low thyroid function.
Cashews	Root, Sacral, Heart	B	Good source of omega-3 and omega-6, vitamins K, B1 and B5, zinc and potassium.
Chestnuts	Root, Sacral, Solar Plexus	B	Reasonable source of B vitamins and vitamin C; low in fat and calories and have less protein and more carbohydrate than other nuts.
Coconuts	Root, Sacral	B	High levels of medium chain saturated fatty acids (MCFAs), including antiviral auric acid (these kinds of saturated fats are metabolized fast in the liver and are less likely to be stored as fat in the body, unlike other saturated fats); coconut oil is good for conditioning the skin and hair.
Hazelnuts	Root, Sacral	B	Good levels of vitamins E, C, and K; omega-3, 6, and 9 (oleic acid); can improve skin, hair, and nails; regulates blood fats; supports the nervous system; helps maintain bone marrow.
Macadamias	Root, Sacral, Heart	B	High in monounsaturated fats, so a rich energy source; can help to lower LDL cholesterol and reduce oxidative stress on the body caused by free-radical damage.
Pecans	Root, Sacral	B	High levels of antioxidants; vitamin E.
Pine nuts	Root, Sacral, Hear	B	Anti-inflammatory; aid metabolism and bone health; may support healthy cholesterol levels and have LDL-lowering properties.
Pistachios	Root, Sacral, Heart, Brow	B	Rich in vitamin B6, which balances hormones; good levels of potassium and fiber, which can help to prevent heart disease; good source of carotenoids lutein and zeaxanthin, which support eye health.
Walnuts	Root, Sacral, Heart, Brow	B	Very rich in antioxidants with a good supply of monounsaturated fats to support cardiovascular health; B vitamins and omega-3 support healthy cognitive function and can aid with sleep.

SEEDS

Seeds, like nuts, are protein rich and tend to contain good levels of essential fatty acids. I often garnish with seeds to add nutrition and texture to a dish, and some nuts act as egg replacers in vegan baking. They all balance the sacral chakra due to their healthy fat content and some work with other chakras, too.

SEEDS	ASSOCIATED CHAKRAS & PURPOSE	EFFECTS	NUTRITIONAL CONTENT AND BENEFITS
Black sesame /tahini	Root, Sacral, Solar Plexus, Heart, Brow	B	High in phytosterols, which help to reduce cholesterol, and magnesium; anti-inflammatory sesamol benefits cardiovascular health; sesame oil helps to prevent diabetes.
Chia	Root, Sacral, Heart, Brow	B	Rich source of Omega-3 and Omega-6 in a ratio of 3:1 (always best to have more 3 than 6); full of protein, vitamins, and minerals; swell when left in water, forming a binding consistency, so egg replacers in vegan baking.
Flaxseed (linseed)	Sacral, Solar Plexus, Heart, Throat, Brow	B	Good source of dietary fiber and omega-3; used to treat coughs and chest infections; useful egg replacer when ground and added to water.
Hemp	Root, Sacral, Heart, Solar Plexus, Brow	B	Rich in Omega-3 and Omega-6 ; helps balance metabolism; protein and fiber can help to regulate digestion and blood-sugar levels; essential amino acids support brain function and maintenance of muscle tissues, cells, and organs.
Pumpkin	Root, Sacral, Heart	B	High levels of zinc, good for skin health; diverse mix of antioxidants; antifungal compound curcubitin alleviates candida; oil of pumpkin seeds may be of benefit to prostate health.
Psyllium husk	Sacral, Solar Plexus, Heart	B	High in fiber; used to regulate digestion and relieve constipation and IBS; helps to reduce cholesterol.
Sunflower	Root, Sacral, Solar Plexus, Heart	B	Rich source of anti-inflammatory vitamin E; good source of phytosterols.

B = Balance | S = Stimulate

GRAINS, FLOURS, AND OTHER GLUTEN-FREE WHOLEFOODS

All grains and flours listed below are wheat and gluten free and some, such as buckwheat and quinoa, are, in fact, not technically grains at all. As carbohydrates, they all stimulate the Solar Plexus chakra. In gluten-free baking, a blend of flours is recommended and I would get used to experimenting in the kitchen with this.

GRAINS & FLOURS	ASSOCIATED CHAKRAS & PURPOSE	EFFECTS	NUTRITIONAL CONTENT AND BENEFITS
Brown rice (basmati) and flour	Root, Sacral, Solar Plexus, Heart	B	Rich in protein, fiber, B vitamins; energy boosting; can help to protect the cardiovascular system; low GI so can help to regulate blood-sugar levels through slow release into the system.
Buckwheat groats and flour	Solar Plexus, Heart	B	Fruit seed; nutty taste; flour is useful in baking, especially when combined with brown rice; good levels of flavonoids and magnesium.
Coconut flour	Root, Sacral, Solar Plexus	B	Protein and fiber rich, dense and filling; best used in small quantities in combination with other flours to add flavor and absorb liquid; see Coconuts (see page 21).
Gram (chickpea) flour	Root, Sacral, Solar Plexus	B	Useful in savory baking; see Chickpeas (see page 17).
Polenta/cornflour (gluten free)	Solar Plexus	S	Low in carbohydrates; rich in vitamins A and C; used to thicken sauces, most often custard, and to help bind in baking; alternative to pasta.
Potato starch	Solar Plexus	S	Thickener and binder used in baking; see Potatoes (see page 16).
Quinoa and flour	Root, Solar Plexus	B	A complete protein; has full spectrum of essential amino acids, which also help the body to form its own proteins; low in carbohydrates and GI, so suitable for diabetics and for regulating blood-sugar levels; alternative to couscous; red and black varieties also available.
Rolled oats and groats	Root, Sacral, Solar Plexus, Heart	B	Rich in dietary fiber; high in B vitamins; groats—the gluten-free whole oat, unadulterated—may have antifungal properties (shown in candida studies); supports cardiovascular health.
Sorghum flour (white, sweet)	Root, Solar Plexus, Heart	B	High in fiber; good level of copper, to help with the absorption of iron (which is also contained within the grass from which the flour is made), supporting circulation and the formation of red blood cells; add to biscuits, pastry, and cakes in small amounts alongside brown rice and buckwheat flours.
Tapioca flour	Root, Solar Plexus, Heart	B	Potassium and iron content can help with regulating the circulatory system and blood pressure; good levels of fiber and protein; thickener, good in custards and sauces; high in carbohydrate, so useful for healthy weight gain.
Teff flour	Root, Solar Plexus, Heart	B	High in protein and rich in nutritional value, containing all the essential amino acids; vitamin C; high levels of calcium, phosphorus, manganese, copper, iron, and aluminum; low in sodium, which can aid heart health; moderate to low GI, which can help to regulate blood-sugar levels.

SWEETENERS

I favor natural and unrefined sweeteners because they have a lower Glycemic Index (GI) than refined sugars (generally a GI of 68), meaning that they won't spike blood-sugar levels, and some are more suitable than refined sugars for diabetics. If sugar is a must, use unrefined raw cane sugar, which is often found in organic vegan chocolate. I've used it in one recipe, as a brûlée topping. All sweeteners stimulate the Solar Plexus chakra; maple syrup and pomegranate molasses also stimulate the root chakra and xylitol the throat chakra.

SWEETENERS	ASSOCIATED CHAKRAS & PURPOSE	EFFECTS	NUTRITIONAL CONTENT AND BENEFITS
Brown rice syrup	Solar Plexus	S	Low GI (25); made from fermented rice; mild, sweet taste and doesn't discolor foods much.
Coconut palm sugar/nectar	Solar Plexus	S	Low GI (35); organic, unprocessed, unbleached (made from dehydrating the blossoms); caramel taste; natural source of B vitamins, iron, potassium, zinc, and magnesium.
Lacuma powder	Solar Plexus	S	Rich in B vitamins and betacarotenes; good source of fiber, minerals, and carbohydrates; extracted from Lacuma fruit; traditionally used in ice cream.
Maple syrup	Solar Plexus, Root	S	Moderate GI (54); made from the sap of the sugar maple tree; medium grade organic syrup processed by evaporation is recommended.
Pomegranate molasses	Solar Plexus, Root	S	Moderate GI (54); made from reducing pomegranate juice; useful in salad dressings.
Stevia	Solar Plexus	S	Herb over 300 times sweeter than sugar (very small amounts needed); combined with xylitol, the edge of after taste is taken off; zero calories and GI, making it suitable for anti-candida diets.
SugaVida™ (palmyra jaggery)	Solar Plexus	S	Low GI (40); good levels of B vitamins (only known plant-generated source of vitamin B12) and iron; harvested from the blossom of the palmyra tree; caramel taste; use 30–50% less than regular sugar.
Xylitol (100% natural)	Solar Plexus, Throat	S	Low GI (7); resembles white sugar in texture and color, but has 40% less calories; toxic to animals; suitable for diabetics in moderation, and for those on an anti-candida diet; good for teeth health; overconsumption can have a laxative effect; always use 100% natural from sustainable plant sources.

B = Balance | S = Stimulate

SUPERFOODS

Superfoods are labeled as such because of their high nutrient content and related health benefits. Here are some that feature in this book and their corresponding chakras.

SUPERFOODS	ASSOCIATED CHAKRAS & PURPOSE	EFFECTS	NUTRITIONAL CONTENT AND BENEFITS
Acai berry powder	Heart, Brow	B	Rich in dietary fiber, calcium, iron, and vitamin E; anthocyanins (antioxidants) excellent for heart health; high ORAC score (Oxygen Radical Absorption Capacity—a measurement of how well antioxidants neutralize free radicals); freeze dried from the berry.
Aloe vera	Sacral, Solar Plexus, Heart, Throat	B	See page 19.
Blueberries	Heart, Brow	B	See page 13.
Chia	Root, Sacral, Heart, Brow	B	See page 22.
Chlorella	Root, Sacral, Heart, Throat	B	See page 18.
Goji berries	Root, Brow	S	Polysaccharides (sugar molecules) increase production of white blood cells; antioxidant lutein supports eye health; used traditionally in Chinese medicine and cuisine to support the immune system.
Maca powder	Root, Sacral, Brow	B	Good mix of fiber, minerals, and carbohydrates; good levels of vitamins B, C, and E, and range of minerals; can be used to boost sexual function and relieve menstrual problems; malty taste, works well on cereals, in hot drinks and smoothies; start with small amounts and slowly build up to around 1 tablespoon per day; created by milling the dried root.
Raw cacao	Heart, Brow	B, S	A top superfood full of essential minerals, including magnesium; B vitamins, antioxidants, fiber, oleic acid, and monunsaturated fats to support heart health; contains "happy" chemicals such as serotonin.
Shiitake mushrooms	Root, Brow	B	See page 16.
Teff quinoa	Root, Solar Plexus, Heart	B	See page 23.

SPRING

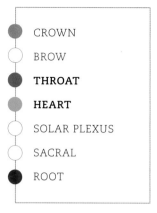

- CROWN
- BROW
- **THROAT**
- **HEART**
- SOLAR PLEXUS
- SACRAL
- ROOT

SERVES 2

SPECIAL EQUIPMENT
slow masticating juicer or blender

1 large cucumber, chopped
2 stalks of celery, chopped, plus extra to garnish (optional)
2 large handfuls of kale, chopped
juice of **2** limes
1 tablespoon kelp powder

Clarity Juice

Speak your truth

I created this green-fuelled savory juice primarily as a heart and throat chakra support. Kelp is an algae rich in iodine so it is great for thyroid and metabolic function; it also contains iron and potassium. This juice is suitable for anti-candida diets.

Put the cucumber, celery, and kale through a juicer, then stir in the lime juice, kelp powder, and ¼ cup/60ml water. Alternatively, blend the lime juice with the other ingredients and pass through a sieve before serving. Drink straight away.

Detox Tea

Spring-clean all the chakras

Having retailed my popular herbal chakra teas Flora and Flame for several years now, I wanted to create a new blend for this book. This tea supports the whole system, but has the primary focus of removing toxins and clearing stagnant energy, preparing you for the summer months. See the nutritional section on pages 19–20 for further information on the individual herbs.

Note: This tea is not suitable for pregnant women.

Combine the herbs and store the tea in an airtight container in the dark, away from direct heat. Use by the "best before" date of the herbs.

To serve, use 1 heaped teaspoon per person and steep in a pot of boiling water for 4–5 minutes. Pour into cups using a tea strainer.

CROWN

BROW

THROAT

HEART

SOLAR PLEXUS

SACRAL

ROOT

MAKES 1¾ oz/50g

½ oz/14g dried red clover
½ oz/14g dried nettle leaves
2 tablespoons dried burdock root
2 tablespoons dried dandelion root

CROWN

BROW

THROAT

HEART

SOLAR PLEXUS

SACRAL

ROOT

MAKES 5 x 8 oz/225g jars

SPECIAL EQUIPMENT
8 x 8 in/20 x 20cm piece of
muslin/cheesecloth; string

4 unwaxed lemons
2½ cups/500g xylitol
juice of **1** lemon
4 tablespoons agar flakes

Low-GI Lemon Marmalade

A guilt-free bit of sunshine!

I was determined to create a simple, bright, and zesty marmalade for spring, but without sugar. This is a runny marmalade, so don't expect it to set to the same level as a pectin-based version.

Boil the jars and their lids in a large pan of water for 10 minutes to sterilize them, then place in the oven on a low temperature to dry.

Wash the lemons and remove the top button-like part. Place in a large saucepan with 5¼ cups/1.25 litres water. Cover and bring to the boil, then reduce the heat and simmer for 1½ hours or until the lemon peel is soft.

Leave to cool, then remove the lemons when touchable. Slice the lemons in half and remove the pips. Place the pips in the center of the muslin and tie with string to form a small bag. Add this to the remaining liquid in the pan.

Cut the peel and flesh of the lemons into strips (as thick or as thin as you like) and add to the pan. Add the xylitol and bring to the boil, stirring until completely dissolved. Semi-cover with a lid and boil rapidly for about 30 minutes.

Prepare the agar by adding the lemon juice and ¼ cup/60ml water to a small pan, then sprinkle the agar flakes on top. Leave to stand for 10 minutes, then bring up to the boil for a few minutes, until the flakes have all dissolved.

Remove the muslin bag from the lemon mix and add the agar liquid, stirring thoroughly, then return to the boil for a further 30 minutes. Leave to cool for 15 minutes, then pour the marmalade into the sterilized jars and seal straight away. Store in the fridge for the best consistency and use within 1 month.

● CROWN
● BROW
● THROAT
● **HEART**
● SOLAR PLEXUS
● SACRAL
● ROOT

SERVES 3–4

1 **head** of broccoli

7 oz/200g collard/spring greens

1 **cup/50g** chopped watercress, plus extra to garnish

3¼ cups/750ml hot vegan stock (made from stock cubes or bouillon cubes/powder)

1 **teaspoon** chlorella powder

½ **teaspoon** freshly ground black pepper

3–4 **tablespoons** mixed seeds

Super Spring Greens Soup

Cleanse your body

I created this recipe when I was following a cleansing anti-candida and parasitic diet, which is great to do during the spring months. Greens formed the bulk of the diet and I found this soup easily digestible. It's a fantastic way to get essential nutrients. Chlorella, an algae, is a great source of iron and Vitamins B6 and B12 and is immune boosting, which makes it excellent to use during a detox. The heart chakra is the primary focus of this dish.

Chop the broccoli and greens. Steam for 5–10 minutes until lightly cooked using either an electric steamer or a colander set over a pan of boiling water, covered with a lid.

Transfer the steamed vegetables to a large mixing bowl and add the watercress. Pour in the hot stock and use a hand blender to combine. Once you have a smooth soup, stir in the chlorella powder and season with black pepper. Serve immediately, garnished with the mixed seeds and extra watercress.

Note: As with many supernutrients, chlorella will lose some of its benefits if overheated, hence adding it at the last minute after the soup has cooled slightly during blending.

Nutty Sprouting Salad

Supernutrients for the body

Spring is the optimum time to eat sprouts, according to ancient Chinese medicine. Get your sprouts going early in the season and you can watch new life unfold before your eyes! The root and heart chakras are primarily supported in this salad with the super-nutritious pea shoots offering a delicate contrast to the denser beans. The sprouts will take a couple of weeks to grow.

Prepare the snow peas by rinsing and letting them stand in a jar of water. Rinse through once or twice a day for 2 days, then drain the snow peas and scatter on the top of the potting compost in the tray (you should only need half the tray for this amount). Leave in a dark place at room temperature for 3 days, watering each morning. On the fourth day, position the tray in a bright room at room temperature, out of direct sunlight. Water once a day and full shoots should be ready to eat within a week. They can be picked and stored in an airtight container in the fridge for up to 1 month.

Sprout the adzuki, mung, and alfalfa by rinsing and placing them in separate sprouting jars or in one sprouter (I have one with three layers and a water tray at the base). Each day rinse them through with fresh water. After 3–4 days they should be ready to eat.

Dry-roast the cashews in a pan over a low heat, then leave to cool for a couple of minutes. Mix the shoots and sprouts together in a salad bowl, add the cashews, and toss through the salad. Prepare the dressing by mixing the oil, vinegar, tamari, and lime juice together, then toss into the salad. Season with black pepper and serve straight away.

Note: If you are not inclined to sprout your own, you can buy a wide variety of fresh sprouts from good wholefood shops. However, the snow pea shoots are harder to find in stores.

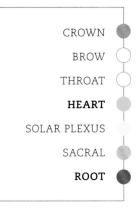

CROWN
BROW
THROAT
HEART
SOLAR PLEXUS
SACRAL
ROOT

SERVES 2

SPECIAL EQUIPMENT
sprouting jars or sprouter; standard seed tray 14 x 9 in/35 x 23cm, filled with organic potting compost

¼ cup/45g snow peas (you can plant more should you wish)
¼ cup/50g dried adzuki beans
1 tablespoon dried mung beans
1 tablespoon alfalfa seeds

SALAD
½ cup/70g cashews
1½ tablespoons sesame oil
1 tablespoon rice vinegar
1 tablespoon tamari sauce
juice of ½ lime
freshly ground black pepper

CROWN

BROW

THROAT

HEART

SOLAR PLEXUS

SACRAL

ROOT

Vegetable Rice Rolls

Asian rainbow of raw foods

Perfect to share as a canapé, appetizer, or light bite, these vegetable rolls are a simple and healthy way to eat the chakra rainbow, supporting your whole system. Spring is a good time of year to increase your raw food intake.

SERVES 4

ROLLS

8 sheets of rice paper

small bunch of scallions/spring onions, finely sliced

½ cucumber, ribboned (using a vegetable peeler)

1 avocado, finely sliced

small bunch of cilantro/coriander, finely chopped

1 carrot, grated

½ red bell pepper, finely sliced

DIP

1 garlic clove, crushed

1 red Thai chili, finely chopped

juice of ½ lime

1 teaspoon rice syrup

Dip the rice papers in warm water to moisten them, then place on a chopping board and allow them to absorb the remaining water for 2 minutes. Use paper towels to dab off any excess water.

Fill the rice papers by spreading each with a lengthwise strip of one-eighth of the scallions/spring onions to form the first layer at the end nearest to you, followed by layers of cucumber, avocado, cilantro/coriander, carrot, and red pepper. Roll up carefully, tucking in the edges as you go, and fold in each end to seal.

Make the dip by combining all the ingredients with 2 tablespoons water in a blender.

Serve the vegetable rolls on a platter, with the dip in the center.

Asparagus and Paprika Tart

All-round chakra support

Nutritional yeast acts as a cheese substitute in sauces and goes well with paprika. Asparagus is prolific in spring, full of vitamin K, and useful for cardiovascular health. This dish supports all the chakras.

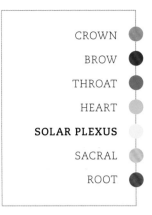

CROWN

BROW

THROAT

HEART

SOLAR PLEXUS

SACRAL

ROOT

To make the pastry, mix the flaxseed with 6 tablespoons water and leave to stand for 10 minutes.

Mix the flours and salt together and add to a food processor with the vegan spread, flaxseed mixture, and walnuts. Mix until a ball of dough is formed. Wrap the dough in plastic wrap and refrigerate for 1 hour.

Preheat the oven to 180°C fan/200°C/400°F/gas mark 6.

Roll out the pastry on a lightly floured surface and line the tart pan (the pastry doesn't need to be too thin—roll until it is just large enough to line the tart pan). Lay parchment paper and pie weights/baking beans on top to weigh down the pastry. Blind bake in the center of the oven for 12–15 minutes. Remove the weights/beans and paper and bake for a further 5 minutes or until the pastry is golden brown. Remove from the oven.

Blanch the asparagus in boiling water for 2 minutes, drain, and set aside to cool. Place the tofu in a blender with half the milk and blend until combined (unlike other recipes in this book, there is no need to press the tofu before use). Add the tofu mixture to a small pan with the parsley, lemon juice, half the paprika, and the remaining milk. Stir and heat until almost at boiling point. Turn off the heat and whisk in the flour until a thick sauce forms. Leave to cool for a minute, then stir in the nutritional yeast and seasoning. Pour the sauce over the pastry base. Decorate with the asparagus tips, placing them in a circle with tips facing inward. Scatter the walnuts over the top. Bake in the oven for 15 minutes.

Remove the tart from the pan and sprinkle with the remaining paprika before serving.

SERVES 4

SPECIAL EQUIPMENT

8 in/20cm loose-bottomed nonstick tart pan; pie weights/baking beans

PASTRY

2 tablespoons ground golden flaxseed

½ cup/80g brown rice flour

⅓ cup/60g buckwheat flour

pinch of sea salt

¼ cup/50g vegan spread

¼ cup/30g walnuts, toasted and roughly chopped

FILLING

16 fine asparagus spears, trimmed

7 oz/200g smoked firm tofu, cubed

⅔ cup/160ml unsweetened plant-based milk

1 teaspoon dried parsley

1 tablespoon lemon juice

1 teaspoon paprika

1 tablespoon tapioca flour

2½ tablespoons nutritional yeast

2 tablespoons chopped walnuts

sea salt and freshly ground black pepper

CROWN

BROW

THROAT

HEART

SOLAR PLEXUS

SACRAL

ROOT

SERVES 2

7 oz/200g smoked firm tofu

large bunch of rainbow chard, chopped

½ cup/60g raw cashews

1 teaspoon paprika

1 teaspoon ground cumin

2 teaspoons nigella seeds

1 tablespoon olive oil

juice of ½ lemon

freshly ground black pepper

Rainbow Chard with Smoked Tofu and Cashews

Quick overall booster

This is a simple, quick, and effortless dish that supports all the chakras. It is perfect when you are in a hurry and want something satisfying yet light. Rainbow chard is always a pleasure on the plate— visually pleasing and full of vitamins A, K, and C.

To prepare the tofu, wrap it in paper towels, then sandwich it between two chopping boards. Weigh down with several large food cans or a heavy book, then leave for 10 minutes to compress and squeeze out any excess water.

Steam the chard for 2–3 minutes.

Slice the tofu and dry-roast with the cashews, paprika, cumin, and half the nigella seeds in a wok or skillet/ frying pan over a low-medium heat for 4–5 minutes, turning regularly.

Add the steamed chard to a separate pan, toss in the olive oil, then stir-fry for 1 minute.

Serve on warmed plates and squeeze over the lemon juice. Garnish with the remaining nigella seeds and season with black pepper.

CROWN

BROW

THROAT

HEART

SOLAR PLEXUS

SACRAL

ROOT

SERVES 4

14 oz/400g can of chopped tomatoes

1 red onion, sliced

1 garlic clove, finely chopped

1 teaspoon ground turmeric

1 teaspoon cumin seeds

1 teaspoon ground cumin

½ cup/75g brown lentils

1 teaspoon garam masala

1 teaspoon ground coriander

½ cauliflower, chopped (including any leaves)

14 oz/400g can of lima/butter beans, drained

2 large handfuls of parsley, chopped, plus extra to garnish

sea salt and freshly ground black pepper

4 tablespoons pumpkin seeds, to garnish

Cauliflower, Butter Bean, and Lentil Curry

Comfort food to warm and ground you

I love this recipe as it requires no additional fats and can be served with either mashed potato or brown basmati rice. This is not a "hot" dish, but good old comfort food to nourish, ground, and fuel your fire through the lower chakras.

Place the chopped tomatoes in a large pan with the onion, garlic, turmeric, cumin seeds, and ground cumin. Stir well and bring to the boil, then simmer for 3 minutes.

Rinse the lentils, then add to the tomato mixture along with the garam masala, ground coriander, cauliflower, and 2 cups/450ml water. Cover and bring to the boil, then reduce the heat and simmer for 20 minutes, stirring occasionally.

If serving with potatoes or rice, prepare and cook these while the curry is cooking.

To toast the pumpkin seeds, preheat the oven to 160°C fan/ 180°C/350°F/gas mark 4. Place the pumpkin seeds on a baking sheet and toast in the oven for 5–7 minutes, turning them halfway through. Remove from the oven and leave to cool.

After 20 minutes, add the lima/butter beans and chopped parsley to the curry, season with salt and pepper, then simmer for a further 5 minutes.

Serve on warmed plates, garnished with the toasted pumpkin seeds and parsley leaves.

CROWN

BROW

THROAT

HEART

SOLAR PLEXUS

SACRAL

ROOT

SERVES 8–10

SPECIAL EQUIPMENT
7 in/18cm springform cake pan,
lightly greased with coconut oil

BASE
1 cup/125g shelled hemp seeds
½ cup/50g raw cacao nibs
¼ cup/20g raw cacao powder
2½ tablespoons coconut nectar
2½ tablespoons coconut oil, melted
and at room temperature

TOPPING
5 avocados, chopped
juice of 6 limes
⅔ cup/150ml coconut oil, melted
and at room temperature
1½ tablespoons coconut nectar or
rice syrup (add slightly more if you
prefer a sweeter taste)

TO DECORATE
1 lime, sliced
1 teaspoon raw cacao nibs, chopped
1 teaspoon raw cacao powder
(optional)

Avocado, Lime, and Raw Cacao Cake

Zesty support for your heart

This cake was in part inspired by those chocolate and lime sweets I adored as a child! I love the combination of tart citrus lime with rich chocolate and wanted to create a raw vegan cake to represent this. The mellow avocado has many health benefits, including a high vitamin E content that supports cardiovascular health. And the raw cacao's mineral-, mood-, and love-boosting chemicals will certainly please your heart chakra!

To make the base, place the hemp seeds, cacao nibs, and cacao powder in a food processor and mix. Add the coconut nectar and coconut oil and process until combined.

Tip the mixture into the base of the prepared cake pan and push down with a spoon until flat and even. Cover the cake pan with plastic wrap and place in the fridge while you prepare the topping.

Place the avocados in the food processor with the lime juice, coconut oil, and coconut nectar or rice syrup. Mix until smooth and creamy in texture, switching to a blender if necessary.

Remove the base from the fridge and pour the avocado topping over it, spreading evenly and smoothly with a spatula. Cover with plastic wrap and place back in the fridge to chill overnight.

To serve, carefully remove from the cake pan and place on a plate. Decorate the cake with lime slices, cacao nibs, and, if you wish, a dusting of cacao powder. Keep the cake refrigerated and eat within 4 days.

● CROWN

● BROW

● THROAT

● HEART

SOLAR PLEXUS

● SACRAL

● ROOT

MAKES 8

INFUSION

2 teaspoons dried dandelion root

2 teaspoons dried burdock root

1½ teaspoons ground star anise

1 teaspoon ground ginger

1 teaspoon xylitol

CAKES

3 tablespoons ground golden flaxseed

½ cup/100ml canola/rapeseed oil

1¼ tablespoons coconut oil, melted and at room temperature

3 tablespoons xylitol

⅛ teaspoon stevia

¾ cup/100g brown rice flour

½ cup/75g buckwheat flour

3½ tablespoons coconut flour

4 teaspoons baking powder

½ cup/125ml dandelion and burdock infusion (*see above*)

TOPPING

1¼ cups/250g xylitol

1½ tablespoons cornstarch/cornflour

¼ cup/50ml (approx) dandelion and burdock infusion (see above)

8 whole star anise, to decorate

Dandelion and Burdock Cupcakes

Cleanse and ground yourself

These are moist, earthy cakes and you can play around with the quantities of flours for a different taste and effect if you wish. Dandelion and burdock roots are great tonics for the digestive system, encouraging flow and cleansing. They work well with the root chakra, grounding and restoring a sense of security.

To make the infusion, place all the ingredients in a saucepan with 2 cups/500ml water and bring to the boil, then reduce the heat and simmer gently for 15 minutes. Turn off the heat and leave to cool to room temperature.

Place the flaxseed in a bowl with ½ cup/135ml water and leave to swell for 10 minutes.

Preheat the oven to 160°C fan/180°C/350°F/gas mark 4. Line a cupcake pan with cupcake liner cases.

To make the cake batter, stir the oils, xylitol, and stevia together in a large bowl. In a separate bowl, mix the flours with the baking powder. Sift the flour gradually into the oil mixture, alternating with the flaxseed mixture, folding in as you go.

Strain the infusion into a measuring pitcher/jug. Pour ½ cup/125ml into the flour mixture, stirring until incorporated. Spoon the mixture into the cupcake liner cases and bake in the middle of the oven for 20–25 minutes or until a skewer inserted into the center comes out clean. Cool the cakes on a wire rack.

Make the topping by grinding the xylitol to a fine powder in a clean coffee grinder. Place in a bowl and mix in the cornstarch/cornflour along with some or all of the remaining infusion until you have a thick frosting (add extra water if necessary). Spoon on to the cooled cakes and leave to set for 10 minutes. Place a star anise on each cake for decoration.

Rhubarb Fool with Ginger Crunch

Stimulate all your chakras

This dessert slips down a treat, and the ginger and lemon combination gives it a lovely kick. Deceivingly filling, a little goes a long way. The ingredients stimulate all the chakras, so it's a "get up and go, bring it on" kind of recipe!

Preheat the oven to 180°C fan/200°C/400°F/gas mark 6.

Chop the rhubarb into ¾ in/2cm slices. Place in a saucepan with the grated ginger, lemon zest and juice, and 5 tablespoons of the xylitol. Bring to a simmer, then cook for 10–15 minutes until the mixture cooks down to a purée, stirring occasionally.

Once the mixture has reached the purée stage, remove from the heat, add the remaining xylitol, and stir well. Tip the purée into a bowl, cover, and leave to cool in the fridge while preparing the topping.

To make the topping, place all the ingredients in a bowl and mix together well. Spread the mixture out on a nonstick baking sheet. Place in the preheated oven for 10–15 minutes until golden brown, turning halfway through, then set aside to cool.

Add the yogurt to the bowl of cooled purée, folding it together until fully combined. Serve in glass dessert bowls, sprinkled with the crunchy topping. If you have any of the topping left, it makes a great breakfast granola.

CROWN

BROW

THROAT

HEART

SOLAR PLEXUS

SACRAL

ROOT

SERVES 3–4 *(or 2 large portions)*

FOOL

1lb 5oz/600g rhubarb

1 tablespoon grated fresh ginger

zest of 1 unwaxed lemon

juice of ½ lemon

½ cup/110g xylitol

1¼ cups/250g unsweetened soya yogurt or coconut yogurt

TOPPING

2 cups/170g gluten-free oats

¾ cup/100g mixed seeds

3½ tablespoons coconut oil, melted and at room temperature

2½ tablespoons maple syrup

1 teaspoon ground ginger

CROWN

BROW

THROAT

HEART

SOLAR PLEXUS

SACRAL

ROOT

SERVES 4

SPECIAL EQUIPMENT

four 3½ in/8cm diameter ramekin dishes

¼ cup/60ml unsweetened plant-based milk

3 tablespoons cornstarch/cornflour

1 tablespoon tapioca flour

1¾ cups/400ml canned coconut milk

3 tablespoons palmyra jaggery/SugaVida™

2½ teaspoons matcha powder

¼ cup/55g unrefined raw cane sugar (golden)

Matcha Brûlée

Awaken your heart and mind

Crème brûlée has long been a favorite dessert of mine and, thanks to this recipe, it can still be enjoyed on a vegan diet. Among its other benefits, superfood matcha is packed full of antioxidants, boosts metabolism, detoxifies, lowers bad LDL cholesterol, and, via the brow chakra, enhances mood and concentration. This creamy delight will liven up any dinner party, but don't eat it too late at night!

Whisk the milk, cornstarch/cornflour, and tapioca flour together in a small bowl.

Heat the coconut milk gently in a pan, stirring in the palmyra jaggery. Bring to simmering point, then pour the flour/milk mixture into the pan, whisking vigorously for about 1 minute until a thick custard is formed. Remove from the heat and leave to cool for 5 minutes, then whisk in the matcha.

Pour into the ramekins and leave to cool for a further 15 minutes, then cover with plastic wrap and place in the fridge to set for 4 hours or until you have a firm to touch custard.

Sprinkle the sugar over the brûlées, then evenly blowtorch them from a distance of 1¼ in/3cm to form a hard top. Cool in the fridge, uncovered, for 5 minutes before serving.

Note: To preserve the nutrients and avoid bitterness, don't add matcha to liquids above 80°C/176°F. You cannot blowtorch palmyra jaggery or coconut palm sugar without them burning, so please don't try as alternatives to the sugar topping.

SUMMER

CROWN

BROW

THROAT

HEART

SOLAR PLEXUS

SACRAL

ROOT

SERVES 2

¾ cup/100g blueberries

1 cup/145g raspberries

8oz/235g strawberries

1 large aloe leaf

1 tablespoon chia seeds

2 teaspoons acai berry powder

Super Berry Smoothie

Morning boost

I recommend this smoothie either for breakfast or before a serious workout, as you will receive a burst of energy to support you from the quick release of sugars broken down in the blending process. The antioxidant-rich superfoods of blueberry, acai, aloe, and chia all provide nutrients to support the skin, energy levels, brain function, digestion, and more. If you aren't keen on the seeds in raspberries, you can blend and strain the juice through a sieve or use a juicer for this part.

Blend all the berries together until they form a thick liquid.

Carefully split the aloe leaf using a small paring knife and scrape the gel from center. Add the gel to the fruit along with the chia seeds, blend for a further 30 seconds, then leave to stand for 10 minutes.

Add the acai berry powder and blend for 30 seconds before serving.

Chilled Pea, Mint, and Avocado Soup

Heartfelt clarity

This soup is pleasant and fresh on a summer's day. It contains mint, which is a great digestive aid, and peas and avocado, which are good digestive and cardiovascular supports (sacral and heart chakras). Water and lemon juice help to bring clarity and boost throat chakra health.

Chop the avocados and blend with the peas, herbs, lemon juice, and 4 cups/960ml water. Season to taste.

Chill in the fridge for 1 hour, then serve with a sprinkling of hemp seeds and fresh mint leaves.

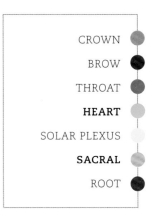

CROWN
BROW
THROAT
HEART
SOLAR PLEXUS
SACRAL
ROOT

SERVES 4

3 avocados

1 cup/125g frozen petit pois, thawed, or fresh peas from the pod

1 tablespoon freshly chopped flat-leaf parsley

2 tablespoons freshly chopped mint, plus extra to garnish

juice of ½ lemon

4 teaspoons shelled hemp seeds

sea salt and freshly ground black pepper

CROWN

BROW

THROAT

HEART

SOLAR PLEXUS

SACRAL

ROOT

Chakra Salad

Taste the rainbow!

This salad is such a simple concept, conceived when I started doing catering at Mind, Body, Spirit events. The rainbow of chakra colors is very pleasing to the eye and lifts the spirits as you eat, uncovering layer by layer, much like discovering the self.

SERVES 6–8

1 **cup plus** 2 **tablespoons/**200g quinoa

4¼ **cups/**1 **litre** vegan stock (made with stock cubes or bouillon cubes/powder)

6 **large** tomatoes, thinly sliced

5 carrots, grated

4 avocados, sliced and tossed in lemon juice

7oz/200g mixed leaves

1 cucumber, thinly sliced

2 **handfuls** of kalamata black olives

2 **small** red onions, sliced, or **handful** of chive flowers

handful of mixed seeds (optional)

DRESSING

2 **tablespoons** balsamic vinegar

⅓ **cup/**80ml olive oil

sea salt and freshly ground black pepper

Rinse the quinoa and place in a pan with the stock. Bring to the boil, then reduce the heat and simmer uncovered for 15–20 minutes, until cooked and the grains are tender. Once cooked, turn off the heat and allow the remaining liquid to be absorbed, then set aside to cool.

Place the tomatoes at the bottom of a glass bowl, or on individual serving plates. Layer the grated carrot on top of the tomatoes. Add the cooled quinoa in a layer, then add the sliced avocados and mixed leaves. Layer the cucumber on next. Finish by sprinkling the olives and the red onion or chive flowers over the top. Scatter over the mixed seeds, if using.

To make the dressing, simply shake or whisk the vinegar and oil together with the seasoning. Pour over the salad and enjoy!

Full of Beans Salad

Try a little tenderness

For this chapter, I wanted to create a simple salad to celebrate the tender sweetness of young beans and peas in the summer months. Legumes are high in fiber and contain a good spectrum of nutrients that can support cardiovascular health. The pomegranate molasses add fruitiness, while the crunchy pine nuts add texture. The heart chakra benefits the most from this dish.

Prepare the quinoa by placing in a pan with the stock, bring to the boil, then simmer, uncovered, for 20 minutes. Take off the heat and allow the excess liquid to be absorbed and the quinoa to cool.

Blanch the fine green beans and fava/broad beans and peas in their pods in separate pans of rolling boiling water for 3–4 minutes. Drain and submerge in bowls of ice-cold water for a further 3 minutes to cool. Pod the fava/broad beans and peas and mix with the green beans in a salad bowl.

Whisk all the dressing ingredients together.

Toast the pine nuts in a dry skillet/frying pan for a couple of minutes over a medium heat. Leave to cool, then toss through the salad with the dressing.

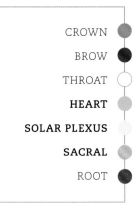

CROWN
BROW
THROAT
HEART
SOLAR PLEXUS
SACRAL
ROOT

SERVES 2–3

½ cup/100g quinoa

2 cups/450ml vegan stock (made from stock cubes or bouillon powder)

3½ oz/100g fine green beans, trimmed

5 oz/150g fresh baby fava/broad beans in the pod

5 oz/150g fresh garden peas in the pod

¼ cup/35g pine nuts

DRESSING

2 tablespoons olive oil

1 tablespoon pomegranate molasses

1 garlic clove, crushed

freshly ground black pepper

CROWN

BROW

THROAT

HEART

SOLAR PLEXUS

SACRAL

ROOT

SERVES 4

2¼ cups/300g dried chickpeas, soaked in cold water overnight
sea salt and ground black pepper

TABBOULEH
1 cup/170g quinoa
2 cups/500ml vegan stock (made from stock cubes or bouillon powder)
1 small red onion
3½ oz/100g baby plum tomatoes
1 red bell pepper
handful of flat-leaf parsley
juice of 1 lime

HUMMUS
4 tablespoons olive oil
2 tablespoons raw tahini
1 garlic clove
juice of 1 lemon
1 teaspoon paprika
1 teaspoon chopped red chili
handful of cilantro/coriander, chopped

SPINACH FALAFEL
2½ cups/75g spinach
7 tablespoons olive oil
1 cup/125g gram flour
½ teaspoon chopped red chili

Quinoa Tabbouleh with Spinach Falafel

A feast for your chakras

A Middle Eastern-themed dish, packed with spice. The highly nutritious, protein- and fiber-rich chickpeas and quinoa support the root and solar plexus chakras to help strengthen and center you.

Rinse the quinoa under running water, then place in a pan with the stock. Bring to the boil, simmer for 20 minutes, then turn off the heat and fork through to distribute any remaining stock—this will be absorbed as the quinoa cools.

Drain the chickpeas from their soaking water and rinse. Place in a pan and cover with water. Bring to the boil and cook for 20 minutes until tender. Drain and rinse under cold water to cool.

To make the hummus, place a third of the cooled chickpeas in a blender with the olive oil, tahini, garlic, lemon juice, paprika, chili, and cilantro/coriander. Add ¼ cup/60ml water and blend well. Season to taste. Tip into a bowl, cover, and place in the fridge.

Prepare the tabbouleh by chopping the onion, tomatoes, pepper, and parsley. Place in a salad bowl and stir through the quinoa. Squeeze over the lime juice and season to taste. Cover and place in the fridge while you prepare the falafel.

To make the falafel, roughly chop the spinach and place in a large bowl. Add the remaining chickpeas, 5 tablespoons olive oil, the gram flour, chili, and 2 tablespoons water and blend with a hand blender. Season to taste. Form into 8 small patties, about 3¼ in/8cm in diameter and ¾ in/2cm thick.

Heat the remaining 2 tablespoons olive oil in a large skillet/ frying pan. Add the falafel to the hot oil (you may need to do this in batches). Fry over a medium heat for 5–7 minutes on each side until well browned and hot all the way through.

Serve with the hummus, tabbouleh, and extra olive oil.

CROWN

BROW

THROAT

HEART

SOLAR PLEXUS

SACRAL

ROOT

Fattoush Salad

Refresh your chakras

I love this traditional Middle Eastern salad with its fresh, zesty flavors—perfect on a hot summer's day. Zatar is a delicious spice blend of sumac, thyme, marjoram, salt, and toasted sesame seeds. It is widely available.

SERVES 4

PITA BREAD

1 teaspoon rice syrup

1 teaspoon dried active yeast

1 tablespoon olive oil

1 teaspoon psyllium husk

½ cup/85g teff flour

½ cup/80g buckwheat groats

¼ cup/45g potato starch

¼ cup/30g tapioca flour

1 teaspoon xanthan gum

½ teaspoon sea salt

2 tablespoons olive oil, for frying

SALAD

1 romaine/cos lettuce

large bunch of scallions/spring onions

3 **large** tomatoes

½ cucumber

handful of mint, chopped

handful of flat-leaf parsley, chopped

DRESSING

3 tablespoons olive oil

juice of 1 lemon

½ red chili, finely chopped

1 garlic clove, crushed

1½ teaspoons zatar

To make the pita, mix the rice syrup with 1 cup/250ml warm water in a bowl, sprinkle on the yeast, and whisk together thoroughly. Place somewhere warm (such as a slightly heated oven, turned off) for 10–15 minutes until the mixture has frothed up.

Stir the oil and psyllium husk into the yeast mixture. Mix all the dry ingredients together, then add to the wet ingredients and stir to form a sticky dough. Cover and leave to prove in a warm place for 1 hour.

Preheat the oven to 200°C fan/220°C/425°F/gas mark 7. Line a large baking sheet with parchment paper.

Turn the dough out onto a lightly floured work surface. Cut into 4 pieces, place on the lined baking sheet, and press down to form ovals about ¼ in/5mm thick. Bake in the oven for 3–4 minutes on one side, then turn over and cook on the other side for a further 3–4 minutes. Remove from the oven and cool on a wire rack.

Finely slice the lettuce and scallions/spring onions, discarding the tougher top green part, and place in a bowl. Chop the tomatoes into small pieces. Slice the cucumber in half and then into matchstick slices. Add both to the bowl with the chopped herbs.

To make the dressing, mix together all the ingredients and set aside for 5 minutes to infuse.

Slice the cooled pita into small strips. Heat the oil in a skillet/frying pan, add the pitas, and fry for 2 minutes on each side. Scatter the hot pita on top of the salad, add the dressing, and toss well.

Green Vegetable Curry

Get to the heart of it

CROWN ●

BROW ●

THROAT ●

HEART ●

SOLAR PLEXUS

SACRAL ●

ROOT ●

A fresh and vibrant curry that primarily supports the heart chakra with potassium-laden fennel, vitamin C-rich green bell pepper, and vitamin K-rich spinach. I like the sweet and bitter combination of flavors of the vegetables with the creamy coconut milk and spices.

SERVES 2

Bring 2 cups/475ml water to the boil in a pan. Rinse the rice and add to the pan of boiling water, then cover and simmer for 20 minutes or until cooked.

Meanwhile, chop the vegetables and cilantro/coriander.

Heat the oil in a large skillet/frying pan or wok and add the spices, followed by the vegetables, and stir-fry over a high heat for a few minutes. Reduce the heat, add the coconut milk and lime juice, and simmer for 5–10 minutes until cooked, stirring occasionally. Season to taste.

Serve with the rice, garnished with the nigella seeds and extra cilantro/coriander.

1 cup/180g brown basmati rice

1 green bell pepper

1 fennel bulb

2 cups/60g spinach

handful of cilantro/coriander, plus extra to garnish

2 tablespoons coconut oil

1 tablespoon grated fresh ginger

2 teaspoons cumin seeds

2 teaspoons ground turmeric

1 cup/250ml coconut milk

juice of 1 lime

sea salt and freshly ground black pepper

2 teaspoons nigella seeds, to garnish

CROWN

BROW

THROAT

HEART

SOLAR PLEXUS

SACRAL

ROOT

Raw Lasagna

A vibrant Mediterranean chakra delight

In a chakra-based recipe book, I just had to add this colorful raw vegan classic with nut "cheese" and Mediterranean flavors. A dish full of nutrients from carotenoid antioxidant-rich tomatoes and spinach to immune-boosting avocados, this is a perfect overall support to the chakra system.

SERVES 4

SPECIAL EQUIPMENT
mandolin

ZUCCHINI/COURGETTE LAYER
2–3 small zucchini/courgettes
¼ cup/60ml olive oil
1 teaspoon sea salt
1 tablespoon chopped oregano

TOMATO LAYER
1 cup/150g sun-dried tomatoes
5oz/150g tomatoes
1 sprig fresh oregano, leaves only
1 teaspoon thyme leaves
1 tablespoon olive oil
1 teaspoon chopped basil
1 garlic clove

SPINACH AND AVOCADO LAYER
1¾ cups/50g spinach, torn
2 avocados
juice of ½ lemon
sea salt and freshly ground black pepper

NUT CHEESE LAYER
1 cup/140g macadamia nuts, soaked in water overnight and drained
½ cup/70g pine nuts
1 tablespoon nutritional yeast
1 teaspoon nutmeg
¼ cup/60ml water
sea salt and freshly ground black pepper

GARNISH
4 sprigs of basil
4 teaspoons pine nuts
1½ cups/175g mixed, herbed, or chili-infused olives

It is best to prepare all the layers of the lasagne before assembling on 4 individual plates.

Begin with the zucchini/courgettes. Remove the ends, then slice thinly using a mandolin. Place in a dish. Mix the olive oil with the salt and oregano, pour over the zucchini/courgettes, and leave to infuse for about 10 minutes while you prepare the remaining layers.

Prepare the tomato layer by processing all the ingredients together until combined, then set aside in a small bowl. Repeat with the spinach and avocado layer, and also the nut cheese layer, processing the ingredients together and setting aside in separate bowls.

Assemble on four individual serving plates. Begin with a layer of three overlapping slices of zucchini/courgette, using paper towels to remove any excess oil. Follow with a thin layer of the tomato mixture, followed by the spinach and avocado, and finally the nut cheese. Repeat all four layers, then finish with a layer of zucchini/courgette.

Garnish with sprigs of basil, a scattering of pine nuts, and a small pot of mixed olives on the side.

CROWN

BROW

THROAT

HEART

SOLAR PLEXUS

SACRAL

ROOT

Stuffed Bell Peppers

Ding dong, bring it on!

I love this colorful and gutsy meal, ideal for a quick and easy light summer lunch or supper. With its fine and intense-flavored stems and leaves, the fantastic celery herb really makes the dish for me, so do try to use it rather than regular celery—it's miles better!

SERVES 2

2 yellow bell peppers

4 stems and leaves of celery herb (or 2 celery stalks)

2 tablespoons sundried tomato paste (or ½ cup/50g chopped sundried tomatoes)

8 cherry plum tomatoes

¼ cup/45g buckwheat groats

2 tablespoons shelled hemp seeds

2 teaspoons celery seeds

drizzle of olive oil

freshly ground black pepper

Preheat the oven to 180°C fan/200°C/400°F/gas mark 6.

Slice the peppers in half, removing the seeds. Place the peppers on a shallow baking sheet with the hollow sides facing up.

Roughly chop the celery and mix with the sundried tomato paste, then spoon into each of the pepper halves. Slice the cherry plum tomatoes in half and place on top of the celery mix.

In a bowl, combine the buckwheat, hemp, and celery seeds, then scatter over the peppers to form a crust. Drizzle with olive oil and season with black pepper. Roast in the preheated oven for 20 minutes.

Serve scattered with chopped celery herb leaves to garnish.

Lentil Moussaka

Greek classic for inner strength

A great favorite of mine, even back in the days when I still ate meat. With its notes of aromatic and stimulating oregano, it is a fantastic warm meal for the summer. The lentils, eggplant/aubergine, and zucchini/courgette balance the solar plexus, while the potato stimulates. A good dish for supporting inner strength, self-esteem, and willpower.

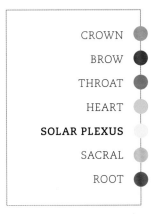

CROWN

BROW

THROAT

HEART

SOLAR PLEXUS

SACRAL

ROOT

Preheat the oven to 160°C fan/180°C/350°F/gas mark 4.

Rinse the lentils, then bring to the boil in a pan of water, cover, and simmer for 20 minutes. Drain and set aside.

Heat the oil in a large pan. Add the onion, garlic, oregano, and cinnamon and sauté over a low heat for 5 minutes, then add the canned tomatoes and the lentils and heat gently for 20 minutes until the juices reduce and the sauce has a thicker consistency.

Prepare the béchamel sauce. Melt the vegan spread in a small nonstick pan, add both flours, and stir to combine. Gradually whisk in the milk and nutmeg over a low heat. Stir until a thick sauce is formed, season with salt and pepper, and remove from the heat.

Blanch the potato in a pan of boiling water for a few minutes. Drain and set aside in a bowl of fresh water.

Cook the eggplant/aubergine and zucchini/courgette slices on a griddle, then set aside.

Drain the blanched potato. Place half the tomato/lentil mixture in the base of the dish, then layer the eggplant/aubergine on top, followed by the zucchini/courgette, the remaining tomato/lentils, and the sliced potato. Pour the béchamel sauce over the top to form a thick layer.

Bake in the center of the preheated oven for 50–60 minutes (cover the top with foil if it browns too quickly).

SERVES 4–6

SPECIAL EQUIPMENT
ovenproof dish approximately 8½ in/ 22cm square and 2½ in/6cm deep

½ cup/100g brown lentils

¼ cup/50g green lentils

2 tablespoons canola/rapeseed oil

1 onion, chopped

2 garlic cloves, chopped

2 tablespoons dried oregano

½ teaspoon ground cinnamon

2 x 14 oz/400g cans of chopped tomatoes

1 large potato, peeled and sliced

1 eggplant/aubergine, sliced lengthwise

1 zucchini/courgette, sliced lengthwise

BÉCHAMEL SAUCE

¼ cup/50g vegan spread

⅓ cup/50g brown rice flour

1½ tablespoons tapioca flour

1¾ cups/400ml unsweetened plant-based milk

1 teaspoon ground nutmeg

salt and freshly ground black pepper

Sunflower Power Cake

Uplift and empower yourself

This cake contains anti-inflammatory chamomile, warming turmeric, and EFA-boosting sunflower seeds, all of which support the solar plexus chakra. This chakra gives us our personal strength.

CROWN ●
BROW ●
THROAT ●
HEART ○
SOLAR PLEXUS
SACRAL ●
ROOT ●

Preheat the oven to 160°C fan/180°C/350°F/gas mark 4. Place the silicone cake mold upside down on a baking sheet.

Grind the chamomile flowers in a food processor or chop finely with a knife. Place in a small bowl, add 1 cup/250ml freshly boiled water, and steep for 10 minutes.

Pour the oil into a medium-size bowl and mix in the coconut palm sugar. Gradually sift in the flours and baking powder, alternating with the flaxseed mixture little by little, folding in until combined. Add the chamomile flowers, their soaking water, and the sunflower seeds and mix well.

Pour the mixture into the cake mold and spread evenly. Bake in the preheated oven for 35–40 minutes. To check the cake is baked, insert a skewer into the center—it should come out clean. Cool in the mold, then place on a serving plate.

To make the topping, place the white chocolate in a large heatproof bowl with the oil. Place the bowl over a pan of simmering water (do not let the bowl touch the water or get water near the chocolate) and stir with a wooden spoon until smooth and runny. Take off the heat, immediately add the turmeric, and quickly stir into the melted chocolate and oil—speed is very important here. Pour the chocolate over the top of the cake, avoiding the center. Spread with the back of a spoon to create a smooth coating. Allow to set.

Place the dark chocolate in a clean heatproof bowl and melt over a pan of simmering water, then remove from the heat and pour into the center of the cake, using the back of a teaspoon to smooth it over the smaller areas. Leave to set for 3–5 minutes, then sprinkle the sunflower seeds over the center of the cake.

SERVES 12

SPECIAL EQUIPMENT

10 in/25cm sunflower-shaped silicone cake mold

CAKE

1½ cups/25g chamomile flowers

¾ cup/200ml sunflower oil

1 cup plus 2 tablespoons/150g coconut palm sugar

1 cup plus 2 tablespoons/150g brown rice flour

¾ cup/100g buckwheat flour

⅓ cup/50g tapioca flour

2 tablespoons baking powder

3 tablespoons ground golden flaxseed, soaked for 10 minutes in ½ cup/125ml water

¾ cup/100g sunflower seeds, roughly chopped

TOPPING

7 oz/200g white vegan chocolate, broken into pieces

1 teaspoon sunflower oil

½ teaspoon ground turmeric

1 oz/25g dark vegan chocolate (72–75% cocoa), broken into pieces

2 teaspoons sunflower seeds

CROWN

BROW

THROAT

HEART

SOLAR PLEXUS

SACRAL

ROOT

Banana, Almond, and Raw Cacao Ice Cream

Sunny days!

This is the most simple vegan ice cream on the planet! I love the banana and chocolate combination and always look for any excuse to get superfood raw cacao into a recipe. This is high in natural sugars and the cacao is also stimulating, so it's best as an occasional treat or when you need extra energy, rather like smoothies.

SERVES 2

5 chopped frozen overripe bananas

⅕ cup/25g whole almonds, plus extra roughly chopped to decorate

⅕ cup/25g raw cacao nibs, plus extra to decorate

Remove the bananas from the freezer and set aside for 5 minutes to thaw slightly.

Place the almonds in a food processor and process until finely chopped, then add the bananas and cacao nibs and mix well.

Serve straight away with a sprinkling of cacao nibs and chopped almonds. (If the ice cream is too slushy after mixing, you can refreeze for an hour or so.)

Chia Pudding with Cardamom and Pistachio

Digestive support

Chia seeds are all the rage as one of the newest superfoods, but they have been used in their native South America for centuries as an aid to digestion and to boost energy. Supporting the root, sacral, and solar plexus chakras, they are loaded with fiber, antioxidants, Omega-3 oils, and lots more. The nuts in this recipe balance the root and sacral chakras, with the cardamom stimulating the solar plexus and brow.

CROWN
BROW
THROAT
HEART
SOLAR PLEXUS
SACRAL
ROOT

SERVES 2

¼ **cup/50g** chia seeds

½ **cup/60g** pistachios, plus **2 tablespoons** roughly chopped to decorate

1 cup plus 1 tablespoon/250ml almond milk

1 teaspoon ground cardamom

coconut nectar or rice syrup, to serve (optional)

Put the chia seeds in a bowl. Roughly chop the pistachios in a food processor. Mix with the milk and cardamom, then stir into the seeds and leave to stand for 15 minutes.

Fork the chia mixture, then cover the bowl and chill for 35 minutes in the fridge. Serve decorated with chopped pistachios. If you wish, add a drizzle of coconut nectar or rice syrup.

CROWN

BROW

THROAT

HEART

SOLAR PLEXUS

SACRAL

ROOT

SERVES 6

SPECIAL EQUIPMENT
ice-cream maker

2 large mangoes, chopped
6 passionfruit (choose dark and
wrinkly ones)
⅓ cup/80ml rice syrup
1 tablespoon lemon juice
good pinch of saffron
(about **15 strands**)

TO DECORATE
¾ cup/35g coconut chips
fresh mint sprigs
seeds from **2** passionfruit

Sexy Summer Sorbet

Balance your center of sexuality

A few years back I created some sexy summer cupcakes and wanted to carry these all-time favorite fruit flavors forward into another summer recipe. Primarily working to balance the sacral chakra, with the saffron adding stimulation, this sorbet may be cold to eat, but could well help to get things heated up in the bedroom!

Blend the mangoes until a smooth purée is formed. Place the mango purée in a sieve and, using a wooden spoon, push the juice through into a bowl. Be sure to scrape as much of the purée as possible from the base of the sieve.

Cut open the passionfruit, scoop out the flesh, and blend for a minute. Sieve the passionfruit purée as above, adding in some of the black seeds at the end for texture, if you wish.

Place the rice syrup, lemon juice, and saffron in a pan with ¼ cup/50ml water, heat gently for a few minutes to encourage the saffron to bleed, then leave the mixture to cool to room temperature.

Pour the syrup mixture and the two purées into the ice-cream maker and churn until firm.

Serve the sorbet on its own or decorated with coconut chips, mint, and extra passionfruit seeds.

Freeze any remaining sorbet in an airtight container; remove from the freezer approximately 10 minutes before serving or until soft enough to scoop.

Note: If you do not have an ice-cream maker, pour the mixture into a shallow airtight container, cover, and freeze until solid ice appears around the sides and base, with a soft slush in the middle. Transfer to a food processor and mix until smooth. Return to the freezer until firm, then mix and freeze twice more.

CROWN

BROW

THROAT

HEART

SOLAR PLEXUS

SACRAL

ROOT

SERVES 6–8

BASE

¼ cup/25g dried goji berries

1½ cups/150g pecan halves

1½ tablespoons raw virgin coconut oil, melted and at room temperature

TOPPING

3½ cups/450g raspberries

2 cups/450g soya cream cheese

1½ tablespoons raw virgin coconut oil, melted and at room temperature

⅓ cup/100ml rice syrup

TO DECORATE

¾ cup/90g raspberries

¼ cup/15g pecan halves

Raspberry, Pecan, and Goji Berry Pudding

Root chakra delight

This dessert is a real treat for any dinner party or gathering (and is best made the day before). It is surprisingly light and full of grounding goodness, with a high content of raspberries, which are known for their anti-inflammatory properties. The layer of fresh fruit in the center works well with the creamy pudding and the dense nutty base to create a well-balanced and textured delight.

Soak the goji berries in a little warm water for 10 minutes, then drain.

To make the base, lightly toast the pecans in a dry pan over a low heat, turning often (this brings out the flavor of the nuts). Place the oil in a food processor with the pecans and goji berries and mix to a granola-type consistency. Spoon the mixture into the base of a medium-size glass dessert bowl, pressing down firmly and spreading evenly, then cover with plastic wrap and place in the fridge.

Place two-thirds of the raspberries in a food processor with the cream cheese and combine. Keeping the machine running on a low setting, gradually add the coconut oil and rice syrup. Once you have a smooth consistency, remove the bowl from the fridge and pour half the mixture over the base, spreading evenly. Add the remaining raspberries as a layer, circling in from the outside and placing the raspberries upside down. Carefully spoon the remaining creamy mixture on top.

Cover once again and place in the fridge overnight. Decorate with raspberries and pecan halves (toasted if you wish) before serving.

FALL

CROWN

BROW

THROAT

HEART

SOLAR PLEXUS

SACRAL

ROOT

MAKES 6

1 cup/125g mixed nuts (such as almonds, walnuts, and brazil nuts)

¼ cup/30g ground golden flaxseed

¼ cup/35g sunflower seeds

1 tablespoon maca powder

2 teaspoons ground cinnamon

⅓ cup/40g dried goji berries

½ cup/100g soft dried figs

½ cup/100g soft dried apricots

½ cup/75g pitted dates

Raw Spiced Energy Bars

A sweet, stimulating treat

These energy bars are seriously moreish and I find it hard to stop myself from eating them. They are packed with balancing protein-filled nuts and seeds alongside stimulating, fiber-rich dried fruits, full of natural sugars. The maca also adds to this energy booster, making them great to eat in the morning or before a workout. The bars will predominantly support your lower chakras.

Pulse the nuts, flaxseed, sunflower seeds, maca, and cinnamon in a food processor for 20 seconds. Add the fruits and process for 1 minute until combined. Remove and place the mixture on a sheet of parchment paper. Place another sheet on top and use a rolling pin to roll the mixture to form an 8 x 4 in/20 x 10cm rectangle.

Cut into six bars, wrap each one in parchment paper, and store in an airtight container in the fridge for 1 hour to firm before serving. Keep refrigerated and enjoy within 1 week.

Note: If you have a nut allergy, try replacing the nuts with the same quantity of buckwheat groats. You must use soft dried figs and apricots as harder dried varieties won't give you a sufficiently sticky consistency.

CROWN

BROW

THROAT

HEART

SOLAR PLEXUS

SACRAL

ROOT

SERVES 2

2 large bananas

1 large pear

1 cup/250ml almond milk

1 tablespoon chia seeds

1 tablespoon shelled hemp seeds

1 tablespoon ground golden flaxseed

⅛ teaspoon cayenne pepper

Warming Smoothie

Fuel your fire

This is a great wholesome morning or pre-exercise smoothie made with potassium-loaded bananas. The warming cayenne really spices up the sweetness of the fruits, firing up the root and solar plexus chakras while also stimulating the brow. The omega-rich three-seed combination works primarily to balance out the sacral chakra.

Peel and slice the bananas, and peel and core the pear. Place in a blender with the almond milk and blend well until smooth. Add the chia, hemp, flaxseed, and cayenne and blend again.

Leave to stand for 5 minutes before serving.

Orchard Hedgerow Juice

Quintessential fall fruits

This simple juice works with countryside fruits from the early part of the season. Blackberries are the first sign that summer is ending and a favorite of my spaniel on our walks! Working to balance the brow chakra, supporting insight, mood, and cognitive function, these indigo fruits are an excellent source of immune-boosting vitamin C, setting you up for the winter.

Peel the apples and pears if you wish and pass them through a juicer whole or chopped, with the blackberries, depending on your machine. Add the lemon juice and ground ginger to the fruit juice and stir well before serving.

Note: If you don't have a juicer, blend the blackberries, apples, and pears (peel and core the latter two first) and pass through a sieve, then add the lemon juice and ginger.

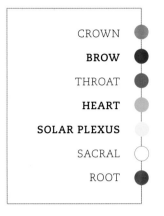

CROWN

BROW

THROAT

HEART

SOLAR PLEXUS

SACRAL

ROOT

SERVES 2

SPECIAL EQUIPMENT
slow masticating juicer

2 **cups/280g** blackberries

3 apples

2 pears

juice of ½ lemon

½ **teaspoon** ground ginger

CROWN

BROW

THROAT

HEART

SOLAR PLEXUS

SACRAL

ROOT

SERVES 4

5 **medium-large** beets/beetroot

2 **large** garlic cloves

1 red onion

2 **tablespoons** olive oil

3 **tablespoons** rosemary leaves

⅓ cup/50g sunflower seeds, plus extra to garnish

2 cups/500ml hot vegan stock (made from stock cubes or bouillon cubes/powder)

sea salt and freshly ground black pepper

Beet and Rosemary Soup

Some flavorsome security

One of my all-time favorites at this time of the year. I grew up eating Grandma's home-grown pickled beets so have always been a fan of this tasty ruby-red plant full of phytochemicals. This is the perfect meal for balancing and stabilizing your root chakra, increasing a sense of security, belonging, and physical wellbeing on earth.

Preheat the oven to 180°C fan/200°C/400°F/gas mark 6.

Peel and chop the beets—you can include the stems as well if you wish, but set them aside in a separate bowl for now.

Slice the garlic and red onion and scatter with the beets in a roasting pan. Drizzle with the olive oil and sprinkle over the rosemary leaves. Roast in the center of the preheated oven for 30 minutes. Leave to cool for 5 minutes.

Toast the sunflower seeds on a baking sheet in the oven for 15 minutes.

Add the roasted vegetables to a food processor with three-quarters of the stock and mix for 1–2 minutes. Transfer the mixture to a blender and add the remaining stock, blending until smooth. Serve straight away or reheat if necessary in a pan. Season to taste and sprinkle with extra sunflower seeds before serving.

Grounding Sweet Potatoes

Extra support for your lower chakras

This is a perfect lunchtime dish, with great flavor synergies between the sweet potato and the black and white bean hummus. Predominantly full of lower chakra-supporting foods, this recipe is good for bringing about the senses of security, creativity, sexuality, emotional balance, and flow. The sweet potato and the beans act as balancing foods for the root, sacral, and solar plexus chakras, while the hint of paprika adds some stimulation to the root and brow chakras.

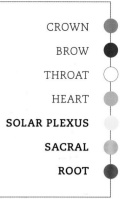

CROWN
BROW
THROAT
HEART
SOLAR PLEXUS
SACRAL
ROOT

Soak the beans for the hummus overnight in two separate bowls of cold water. The next day, drain and rinse. Place the lima/ butter beans in a pan of water, boil for 15 minutes, then cover and simmer for 1½ hours. Put the black beans in a separate pan of water, boil for 15 minutes, then cover and simmer for 40 minutes. When cooked, drain both pans and allow the beans to cool.

Preheat the oven to 180°C fan/200°C/400°F/gas mark 6.

Place the whole sweet potatoes on a baking sheet and toss with the olive oil and a little salt. Bake in the preheated oven for 45 minutes until soft.

Meanwhile, make the hummus. Put the beans in a food processor with the rest of the ingredients, mixing until you have a chunky but smooth consistency. If necessary, use a spatula to scrape any stuck mixture from the sides of the processor bowl and add a little more oil or water to moisten the mixture if it is too dry. Season to taste.

When ready to serve, cut the sweet potatoes in half lengthwise and spoon the hummus over generously. Scatter with pumpkin seeds and serve with a spicy leaf garnish.

SERVES 6

6 sweet potatoes
1 teaspoon olive oil
½ teaspoon salt

BLACK AND WHITE HUMMUS
¾ cup/120g dried lima/butter beans
⅔ cup/120g dried black turtle beans
2 teaspoons ground cumin
1 teaspoon paprika
1 tablespoon freshly squeezed orange juice
1 tablespoon freshly squeezed lemon juice
2 tablespoons olive oil
1 tablespoon raw tahini
sea salt and freshly ground black pepper

TO GARNISH
pumpkin seeds
mixed spicy salad leaves

CROWN

BROW

THROAT

HEART

SOLAR PLEXUS

SACRAL

ROOT

SERVES 4

2 **tablespoons** coconut or canola/
rapeseed oil

1 red onion, chopped

2 garlic cloves, chopped

4 **teaspoons** ras el hanout (see note)

1 **cup/225g** amaranth

1½ **cups/200g** dried chickpeas,
soaked overnight in cold water

1 **large** sweet potato, cubed

1 pumpkin—you will need
1 **lb 10 oz/735g** cubed flesh

¼ **teaspoon** sea salt

½ **cup/65g** raisins

1 **cup/90g** toasted slivered/flaked
almonds

sea salt and freshly ground black
pepper

sprigs of cilantro/coriander, to
garnish (optional)

Moroccan Pumpkin Stew

Spark your creativity and personal power

I love spices for their fragrance and health benefits and this North African-influenced dish is a great way to introduce a sweetness that negates the craving for dessert. You can easily purchase ras el hanout spice blend or make your own, as below. The sacral and solar plexus chakras are supported predominantly with balancing pumpkin and protein- and mineral-rich amaranth and chickpeas.

Gently heat the oil in a large pan, add the onion, garlic, and spice and sweat over a low heat for 5 minutes.

Meanwhile, put the amaranth into a pan with 2 cups/500ml water. Bring to the boil, then simmer for 20 minutes. Take off the heat and allow any remaining water to be absorbed (I like it a bit crunchy and couscous-like in texture, hence cooking for a shorter time than some may suggest).

Drain the chickpeas and add with the chopped sweet potato and pumpkin to the pan containing the onions. Add 3 cups/750ml water, cover, and simmer for 15 minutes. Stir thoroughly, then add the salt and raisins and simmer for a further 5 minutes.

Season the amaranth to taste and stir in three-quarters of the almonds. Serve with the pumpkin stew, garnished with the remaining almonds and sprigs of cilantro/coriander.

Note: To make your own ras el hanout spice mix, in a dry pan toast 3 tablespoons cumin seeds, 2½ tablespoons coriander seeds, 1½ tablespoons ground cinnamon, 2½ teaspoons ground ginger, 2 teaspoons black peppercorns, 1½ teaspoons ground turmeric, 1 teaspoon paprika, ½ teaspoon cardamom seeds, ½ teaspoon ground nutmeg, ¼ teaspoon cloves, and a pinch of saffron threads for a few minutes until fragrant. Grind in a spice grinder or clean coffee grinder with a few dried rose petals. Store any leftover spice mixture in an airtight jar.

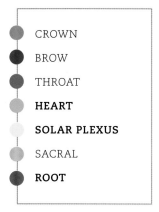

CROWN

BROW

THROAT

HEART

SOLAR PLEXUS

SACRAL

ROOT

SERVES 2

¾ cup/10g dried shiitake mushrooms

2 tablespoons olive oil

1 garlic clove, crushed

¾ cup/150g arborio rice, rinsed in cold water and drained

1¾ cups/400ml vegan stock (made from stock cubes or bouillon cubes/ powder with freshly boiled water and the mushroom soaking water)

½ teaspoon chopped red chili

½ large leek, chopped

1¾ oz/50g kale, chopped

2 tablespoons dried goji berries

freshly ground black pepper

2 teaspoons pumpkin seeds, to garnish

Leek, Kale, and Mushroom Risotto

A hearty meal!

I adore risotto and all things Italian, so wanted to create a green version for an extra boost to the heart chakra. Leeks contain the flavonoid kaempferol and antioxidant polyphenols, which can help to protect the cardiovascular system. The hint of color and sweetness from the goji berries adds an unusual dimension and these little superfood wonders complement the shiitake mushrooms to provide a nutritious, immune-boosting dish.

Place the mushrooms in a small bowl, cover with freshly boiled water, and leave to soak for 20 minutes.

Gently heat the oil in a large pan. Add the crushed garlic and rice with a quarter of the stock, bring up to a gentle simmer, and stir until the stock is absorbed. Add the chopped chili and leek and repeat with a further quarter of the stock. Once absorbed, add the remaining stock with the kale and goji berries and stir until the stock is absorbed and you have a creamy risotto.

Season with black pepper and serve with a scattering of pumpkin seeds.

Spaghetti Squash with Tofu, Nori, and Kale Pesto

Complete chakra nourishment

An excellent, lighter alternative to pasta, spaghetti squash is full of fiber and low in carbohydrates. The pesto is packed with chlorophyll-containing ingredients, including vitamin- and mineral-rich nori. This works well with the tofu to create a satisfying protein-based meal that supports all seven chakras.

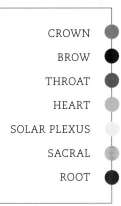

CROWN
BROW
THROAT
HEART
SOLAR PLEXUS
SACRAL
ROOT

SERVES 4

1 **large** spaghetti squash

½ **cup/100ml** olive oil, plus **2 extra** tablespoons

½ **teaspoon** sea salt

1 **teaspoon** dried Italian herbs (such as a mixture of thyme, oregano, marjoram, and rosemary)

14 oz/400g smoked or herb-marinated tofu

¼ **cup/35g** pine nuts, plus extra toasted to garnish

1¼ oz /35g kale

⅓ oz/10g dried green nori (sheets or sprinkles)

1¼ oz/35g basil

juice of ½ lemon

2 garlic cloves

2 **tablespoons** shelled hemp seeds

freshly ground black pepper

Preheat the oven to 200°C fan/220°C/425°F/gas mark 7.

Prepare the squash by slicing in half lengthwise. Scoop out the seeds and the central flesh. Place both halves on a baking sheet, hollow side up, and drizzle over 2 tablespoons of olive oil, plus salt and pepper to taste. Scatter the dried herbs over the squash (if you prefer to use fresh herbs, chop finely before adding). Roast in the preheated oven for 35 minutes.

Meanwhile, prepare the tofu by draining it, then wrapping in paper towels. Place between two chopping boards, weigh it down (such as with heavy food cans), and leave for 10 minutes until pressed firm.

Dry-roast the pine nuts in a pan over a medium heat, tossing until brown on all sides. Place in a food processor with the kale, nori (tear into smaller pieces if using the sheets), basil, lemon juice, garlic cloves, hemp seeds, and the remaining olive oil and process until the pesto reaches a coarse consistency.

Slice the tofu ¼ in/5mm thick, place on a nonstick baking sheet, and roast in the oven for 8–10 minutes.

Use a fork to scrape the flesh of the squash into spaghetti strands, toss with the pesto and tofu, and serve on warmed plates. Season to taste with black pepper and garnish with extra toasted pine nuts.

CROWN

BROW

THROAT

HEART

SOLAR PLEXUS

SACRAL

ROOT

SERVES 4

1 **large** red onion

3 **large** potatoes

1 **large** cauliflower

2 **tablespoons** coconut oil

1 **teaspoon** cumin seeds

1 **teaspoon** nigella seeds

1 **teaspoon** ground turmeric

2 garlic cloves, sliced

⅓ **cup/50g** mixed seeds

sea salt and freshly ground black pepper

Roasted Cauliflower and Potato Crunch

You can do it!

This is one of my favorite quick meals for this time of the year when I crave roasted veg. The spices and potato stimulate your solar plexus center of power and transformation, while the cauliflower works to balance this area and the heart. A great dish for comfort and reassurance.

Preheat the oven to 200°C fan/220°C/425°F/gas mark 7.

Cut the onion, potatoes, and cauliflower into chunks.

Place the coconut oil in a roasting pan and melt briefly in the oven, then add vegetables, all the spices, and seasoning. Roast at the top of the oven for 45 minutes, adding the garlic and mixed seeds halfway through and tossing through the vegetables.

Serve with a tasty organic chutney or pickle.

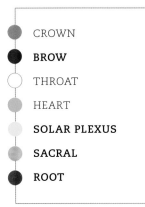

CROWN

BROW

THROAT

HEART

SOLAR PLEXUS

SACRAL

ROOT

SERVES 4

SPECIAL EQUIPMENT
mini food processor or coffee grinder

1 cup/125g raw cashews

½ cup plus 1 tablespoon/90g brown rice flour

3½ tablespoons tapioca flour

¼ cup/30g sorghum flour

1 tablespoon baking powder

1 teaspoon ground cinnamon

1 teaspoon ground ginger

½ teaspoon freshly grated nutmeg

pinch of ground cloves

pinch of sea salt

⅓ cup/40g raisins or golden raisins/sultanas

¾ cup/180ml unsweetened plant-based milk

Spiced Fruit Scones

Traditional English treat made healthy

I grew up on scones and found the salt and refined sugar-laden shop-bought kind to be unappealing. Nothing beats a light home-baked scone and these are full of nourishing nuts, wholegrains, spices, and fruits. These predominantly support the root, solar plexus, and brow chakras through stimulating and balancing ingredients.

Preheat the oven to 200°C fan/220°C/425°F/gas mark 7.

Grind the cashews into a flour using a mini food processor or coffee grinder. Place the flour in a mixing bowl with the other dry ingredients and the dried fruit. Create a well in the center and pour in the milk, then gradually incorporate using a wooden spoon. Once you have a sticky mixture, spoon the mixture on to a nonstick baking sheet in four mounds 1¾–2in/4–5cm in height.

Place in the center of the oven and bake for 20 minutes until slightly browned on the top.

Cool on a wire rack for 15 minutes, then serve warm with vegan spread and/or low G-I jam.

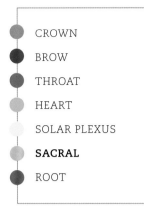

CROWN

BROW

THROAT

HEART

SOLAR PLEXUS

SACRAL

ROOT

SERVES 8–10

SPECIAL EQUIPMENT
7 in/18cm nonstick springform
cake pan

BASE
¼ cup/35g golden flaxseeds
¾ cup/100g whole almonds
1½ cups/200g soft dried apricots

FILLING
6 oz/175g butternut squash
6 oz/175g carrots
¾ cup/100g soft dried apricots
zest and juice of 2 oranges
⅓ cup/100ml coconut oil, melted
and at room temperature
½ cup/50g ground almonds
3 tablespoons coconut nectar syrup
1 teaspoon ground cinnamon

TOPPING
1½ cups/350ml orange juice, strained
1½ tablespoons agar flakes
1 tablespoon coconut nectar syrup

TO DECORATE
1 long, straight carrot, for the roses
2 tablespoons xylitol
¼ cup/40g whole almonds

Sacral Bliss Cake

Get passionate, get creative

This is a dense and sweet 95% raw vegan cake packed with mainly sacral chakra-boosting and balancing ingredients, getting almost all its sweetness from the fruits and vegetables it contains. The apricots are the most stimulating, so if you have an overactive sacral chakra and want to create a completely balanced cake, cut down on these in the filling and replace with more carrots, squash, and coconut nectar for sweetness. This cake requires setting in the fridge overnight.

First make the base. Put the flaxseeds in a blender and pulse for 1 minute. Place the almonds in a food processor with the apricots and ground flaxseeds, pulsing until small pieces are formed, like a sticky granola. Tip the base mixture into the cake pan and press down with the back of a spoon until a smooth, flat surface is formed. Cover with plastic wrap and place in the fridge.

To make the filling, peel and grate the butternut squash (discard the seeds) and carrots into a food processor (or use a grating attachment on the food processor, if you have one). Add the remaining filling ingredients and mix well. When as smooth as possible, decant into a blender and mix until very smooth. Take the base out of the fridge and pour the filling mixture over the top. Spread it out evenly, then loosely cover with plastic wrap and place in the fridge overnight.

The next day, prepare the jelly topping. Place the ingredients in a small pan and bring to the boil, then reduce the heat and simmer for 10 minutes, stirring occasionally, until all the agar flakes are dissolved. Pour the mixture into a glass pitcher/jug and leave to cool for 20 minutes.

Take the cake pan out of the fridge and pour the cooled liquid jelly over the top of the cake. Cover with plastic wrap again and place back in the fridge for 1 hour to set.

Meanwhile, prepare the carrot roses. Peel the carrot and create a flat edge by slicing with a knife. Use a vegetable peeler to peel long, thin slices of carrot and set aside.

Place the xylitol in a small nonstick pan with 1½ tablespoons water. Bring to the boil, then reduce to a simmer. Add the slices of carrot and simmer for 1 minute, then turn off the heat and leave the carrot slices to cool in the syrup.

Once cool, carefully remove one of the carrot strips and gently shake off the excess syrup.

Hold one end and form a small twist (this will be the center of the rose), then wrap around the rest of the strip using a twisting formation as you go. Place the finished rose on parchment paper and repeat with the other strips.

Remove the cake from the fridge and decorate with the carrot roses and almonds before serving. Keep refrigerated and eat within 4 days.

CROWN

BROW

THROAT

HEART

SOLAR PLEXUS

SACRAL

ROOT

SERVES 4

SPECIAL EQUIPMENT
four 4 in/10cm loose-bottomed nonstick tart pans; pie weights/baking beans

PASTRY
¼ cup/40g brown rice flour

2 tablespoons buckwheat flour

2 tablespoons coconut flour

1 tablespoon sorghum flour

½ tablespoon tapioca flour

pinch of sea salt

2 tablespoons vegan spread

2½ tablespoons hazelnut butter

2 tablespoons unsweetened plant-based milk

CUSTARD
½ vanilla bean/pod

2 cups/480ml unsweetened plant-based milk, plus **2 tablespoons**

2 tablespoons rice syrup

3 tablespoons cornstarch/cornflour

FILLING
4 large red plums

2 tablespoons chopped hazelnuts

½ teaspoon caraway seeds

Hazelnut Plum Tart

Fall fruit-and-nut delight

Hazelnuts and plums bring a balanced, grounding aspect to this dish, while caraway stimulates and acts as a tonic to the body, aiding digestion. Vanilla custard adds warmth to the solar plexus and grounding through the maple syrup. Root and solar plexus are the main chakras supported by this tart.

To make the pastry, combine the flours and salt, then place in a food processor with the vegan spread, hazelnut butter, and milk. Once a dough ball is formed (you can use your hands at this stage to help if necessary), wrap in plastic wrap and place in the fridge for 30 minutes.

Preheat the oven to 170°C fan/190°C/375°F/gas mark 5.

Roll the dough out on a lightly floured surface to a thickness of ¼ in/5mm. Cut out circles of dough slightly larger than the tart pans. Line each pan with pastry, molding it to the fluted edge (it is best to lift the circles using a spatula to prevent breakage). Line the pastry shells with parchment paper and pie weights/baking beans, then place on a baking sheet. Bake in the center of the oven for 5 minutes, then set aside.

To make the custard, split the vanilla bean/pod open and scrape out the seeds. Place in a pan with the main quantity of plant milk and the rice syrup and heat to simmering point. Place the cornstarch/cornflour in a small bowl, add the extra 2 tablespoons milk, and mix to a paste. Whisk the paste into the vanilla milk over a low-medium heat until a custard is formed. Take off the heat.

Remove the plum pits/stones. Slice the fruit into half moons.

Pour ¾ cup/180ml of the custard into the pastry shells, then arrange the plums on top, overlapping them with the skin side facing upward. Scatter over the hazelnuts and caraway seeds. Bake in the oven for 25 minutes, then leave to cool for a few minutes before removing from the pans. Serve warm with the rest of the custard (reheated if you wish).

CROWN

BROW

THROAT

HEART

SOLAR PLEXUS

SACRAL

ROOT

SERVES 4–6

¾ cup/135g brown basmati rice

4 cups/950ml almond milk

⅓ cup/45g chopped almonds

1 tablespoon maca powder

2½ tablespoons maple syrup

TO DECORATE

maple syrup

freshly grated nutmeg

toasted slivered/flaked almonds

Almond Rice Pudding

Harmonize your lower chakras

A good old favorite in the English kitchen, rice pudding is another great way to support and reassure through the lower chakras, especially with the inclusion of almonds and superfood maca. I like to use brown rice whenever possible as it is unprocessed, keeping its nutrients—such as manganese, selenium, B vitamins, and phosphorus—intact.

Preheat the oven to 130°C fan/150°C/300°F/gas mark 2.

Rinse the rice under cold running water and place in an ovenproof dish with the almond milk. Cover with foil and cook in the center of the oven for 1¼ hours.

Remove from the oven and leave to cool for 10 minutes.

Stir through the chopped almonds, maca, and maple syrup. Serve with a drizzle of maple syrup, and topped with a grating of fresh nutmeg, and a scattering of toasted almonds.

Baked Pears with Cinnamon and Blackberries

Synchronize your heart and mind

A simple and deliciously warming pudding, full of autumnal fruity goodness with a hint of sweet spice. Pears support the heart chakra, whilst the injection of color from the blackberries balances out the brow, meaning this dish may well help to put your heart and mind on the same page!

CROWN

BROW

THROAT

HEART

SOLAR PLEXUS

SACRAL

ROOT

SERVES 2

2 ripe green pears
1 teaspoon ground cinnamon
1 tablespoon raw coconut nectar
1 cup/150g blackberries

Preheat the oven to 160°C fan/180°C/350°F/gas mark 4.

Slice each pear in half and scoop out the core using a spoon. Place the pears in a row on a foil-lined baking sheet (cut a piece of foil large enough to form a parcel around the pears).

Mix the cinnamon with the coconut nectar in a small bowl. Add a handful of the blackberries to the center of each pear, followed by a good sprinkling of the cinnamon mixture. Fold up the sides of the foil to form a parcel, sealing it at the top. Bake in the center of the oven for 25–30 minutes.

Once the pears are soft to touch and the juices are flowing, remove from the oven and serve two halves per person in shallow bowls. Carefully pour over any juices left in the foil parcel.

CROWN

BROW

THROAT

HEART

SOLAR PLEXUS

SACRAL

ROOT

SERVES 2

2½ cups/600ml unsweetened plant-based milk

1 teaspoon ground cardamom

1 teaspoon ground cinnamon

½ teaspoon ground ginger

½ teaspoon freshly grated nutmeg, plus extra to serve

¼ teaspoon ground cloves

¼ teaspoon freshly ground black pepper

Chai Latte

Spice up your life!

I just love making this simple and tasty homage to the spice world. I don't feel the need to add sweetener here, as the spices and plant milk work their magic. This drink is warming and stimulating for the chakras concerned, so I find it is perfect as a mid-afternoon restorative after a long walk with my dog.

Pour the plant milk into a small saucepan and gently heat as you stir in all the spices. Bring almost to simmering point, whisking as the milk heats, then pour into two large cups or mugs.

Dust with a little freshly grated nutmeg before serving.

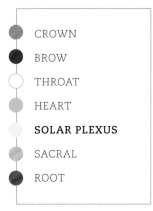

- CROWN
- BROW
- THROAT
- HEART
- **SOLAR PLEXUS**
- SACRAL
- ROOT

Wake-me-up Porridge

Kickstart your day

This porridge is a favorite of mine, with warming, stimulating ginger and nutrient-packed superfoods maca and chia. It really does feed and balance the solar plexus chakra, with the slow-release carbohydrates from the oats keeping you satisfied throughout the morning. I have included a cooked and a raw version of this recipe.

SERVES 2

1 cup/90g gluten-free oats
(sprouted if possible)

2½ cups/600ml unsweetened
plant-based milk

2 tablespoons chia seeds

2 teaspoons ground ginger

2 teaspoons maca powder

2 tablespoons desiccated coconut

2 tablespoons shelled hemp seeds

2 tablespoons raw cacao nibs

Place the oats and the milk into a small saucepan and heat gently for 3–4 minutes, stirring until you have a loose, milky porridge—do not allow it to reach boiling point.

Turn off the heat and add the chia seeds, stir well, then leave swell and cool for 2 minutes. Add the ginger and maca and half the coconut, hemp, and cacao nibs and mix well. It is important not to add the maca at a high temperature as it would lose some of its nutrients.

Spoon into two bowls and sprinkle the remaining coconut, hemp seeds, and cacao nibs on top before serving.

Note: For a raw version of this porridge, soak 1 cup/170g raw gluten-free oat groats overnight in 2 cups/500ml water. The following morning, blend the groats and water with the chia, ginger, maca, and coconut. Leave to stand for 5 minutes, then serve with the hemp and cacao nibs scattered on top.

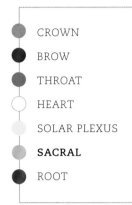

CROWN

BROW

THROAT

HEART

SOLAR PLEXUS

SACRAL

ROOT

Sacral Juice

Go with the creative flow

This simple spiced version of an old classic will support your sacral center of creativity and passion with balancing carrots and stimulating oranges and nutmeg.

SERVES 2

5 carrots
juice of 4 oranges
½ **teaspoon** nutmeg
¼ **teaspoon** paprika

Peel and juice the carrots. Add the freshly squeezed orange juice and stir in the spices. Serve straight away in two glasses.

Three Squash Soup

A right royal soup!

This soup celebrates three of my favorite squash varieties, but you can substitute others if these are not available. The contrast of sweet and nutty flavors is delicious, working well with paprika to create a satisfying vitamin A-packed soup to primarily support the sacral, solar plexus, and throat chakras.

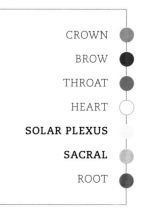

CROWN
BROW
THROAT
HEART
SOLAR PLEXUS
SACRAL
ROOT

SERVES 4

Preheat the oven to 200°C fan/220°C/425°F/gas mark 7.

With some squash varieties you can eat the skin, so check this before preparing. Cube the squash (peeling where necessary), and discard the inner seeds. Place in a large roasting pan and toss in the olive oil. Roast for 35 minutes, turning halfway through.

Once the squash is cooked, transfer to a large bowl. Add the stock and paprika and use a hand blender to combine until smooth. Season and add more water to thin as required. Reheat if necessary, season with black pepper, and scatter with pumpkin seeds to serve.

½ crown prince squash

½ uchiki kuri (red onion squash)

¼ Turk's turban squash
(you need approx 1¾ lbs/800g squash flesh in total)

1½ tablespoons olive oil

3¼ cups/750ml hot vegan stock
(made from stock cubes or bouillon cubes/powder)

1 teaspoon paprika

freshly ground black pepper

pumpkin seeds, to garnish

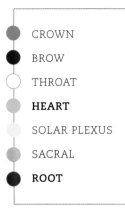

CROWN

BROW

THROAT

HEART

SOLAR PLEXUS

SACRAL

ROOT

SERVES 4

1 large beet/beetroot
1 large carrot
¼ celeriac
¼ red cabbage
1 tablespoon mustard
2 tablespoons olive oil
2 tablespoons apple cider vinegar
1 tablespoon caraway seeds
2 tablespoons sunflower seeds
sea salt and freshly ground black pepper

Winter Slaw

Colorful crunch for the darker months

This tasty winter slaw brings together some beautiful and nutritious vegetables full of color. It primarily supports the root and heart chakras through the balancing beet, carrot, red cabbage, and celeriac. The flavorsome antioxidant and mineral-rich caraway seeds add depth and sweetness to the dish.

Peel and grate the beet, carrot, and celeriac into a bowl (use a food processor if you have the relevant attachment). Finely slice the cabbage and add to the bowl.

Mix the mustard, olive oil, and vinegar together with seasoning to form the dressing. Toss this into the slaw with the caraway seeds and serve with the sunflower seeds scattered on top.

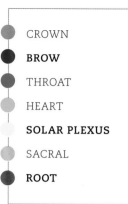

CROWN

BROW

THROAT

HEART

SOLAR PLEXUS

SACRAL

ROOT

SERVES 4

WINTER ROOTS

3 carrots

2 parsnips

2 **large** beets/beetroot

1 **small** celeriac

1 **large** red onion

2 garlic cloves

2 tablespoons canola/rapeseed oil

cilantro/coriander leaves, to garnish

PATTIES

¾ cup/125g dried kidney beans, soaked in cold water overnight and drained

¼ cup/50g French or brown lentils

1¾ oz/50g kale, chopped

4 tablespoons rapeseed oil

juice of ½ a lemon

½ cup/60g ground golden flaxseed

½ teaspoon chili powder

½ teaspoon ground turmeric

1 teaspoon cumin seeds

½ teaspoon ground cumin

1 teaspoon ground coriander

1½ teaspoons sea salt

freshly ground black pepper

Spiced Patties with Roasted Winter Roots

Grounding winter warmth

A great comfort food recipe for the winter months, packed with Indian spices and flavorsome root vegetables. This is a highly nutritious and filling dish full of dietary fiber from the legumes, kale, and roots. It will primarily support the root, solar plexus and brow chakras.

Rinse the beans in fresh water. Place in a pan of water and boil rapidly for 10 minutes, then simmer for 1¼ hours. Drain and set aside.

Rinse the lentils, place in a pan of water, bring to the boil, then simmer for 30 minutes. Drain and set aside.

Preheat the oven to 180°C fan/200°C/400°F/gas mark 6.

Peel and chop the carrots, parsnips, beets, celeriac, and onion into chunks, then place in a roasting pan. Crush the garlic over the top of the vegetables and drizzle with the oil. Roast for 35 minutes, turning halfway through.

To make the patties, process the kale in a food processor until finely chopped. Mash the beans and lentils together with half the oil, the lemon juice, spices, and salt. Add pepper to taste. Combine with the kale and half the flaxseed in a food processor for 1–2 minutes. Divide into four patties and coat each in the remaining flax.

Heat the remaining oil in a shallow skillet/frying pan. Carefully transfer the patties into the pan (they are quite soft and delicate) and fry for 4–5 minutes on each side over a medium heat.

Serve the patties with the roasted veg. scattered with cilantro/coriander leaves. I recommend serving this dish with an organic fruit chutney, such as mango or peach.

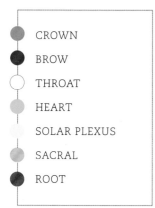
SERVES 4

3½ oz/100g brown rice noodles

3 tablespoons canola/rapeseed oil

1 red onion, chopped

1 garlic clove, crushed

10½ oz/300g Brussels sprouts, sliced

2 Jerusalem artichokes, sliced

½ teaspoon finely chopped red chili

1 tablespoon grated fresh ginger

2 tablespoons dried goji berries

TO GARNISH

2 tablespoons sesame oil

tamari sauce, to taste

2 tablespoons chopped walnuts

Brussels Sprout and Artichoke Stir-Fry

Seasonal favorites with an Asian twist

I wanted to create a seasonal stir-fry with two of my favorite crisp and crunchy vegetables—Brussels sprouts and Jerusalem artichokes. The latter balance the root and solar plexus chakra and contain the prebiotic inulin that can help support probiotics in the body for better digestion and all-round good health. In the stir-fry they add a welcome texture.

To cook the rice noodles, place in a pan of boiling water and simmering for the time indicated on the package (usually 5–8 minutes).

While the noodles are cooking, heat the oil in a wok. Add the onion and garlic and stir-fry for 1 minute over a high heat. Add the Brussels sprouts and artichokes and continue to stir-fry for 5 minutes, then add the chili, ginger, and goji berries and stir-fry for a further 3 minutes.

Drain the noodles and either stir through the vegetables before serving or serve the vegetables on top of them. Drizzle with the sesame oil, add tamari sauce to taste, and scatter with the walnuts.

CROWN

BROW

THROAT

HEART

SOLAR PLEXUS

SACRAL

ROOT

Rooty Daal with Sweet Naan Bread

Comfort your lower chakras

This is one of my all-time favorites for the winter months. It is a bowl of colorful hugs for your lower chakras, combined with a naan containing nigella seeds and golden raisins/sultanas that also support your throat and brow chakras.

SERVES 4

DAAL

3 large potatoes

3 carrots

2 large parsnips

1 red onion

2 garlic cloves

2 tablespoons coconut oil

1 teaspoon finely chopped red chili

2 teaspoons ground turmeric

1 teaspoon garam masala

⅔ cup/125g green lentils (choose those that don't require presoaking)

2⅓ cups/550ml vegan stock (made with stock cubes or bouillon cubes/powder)

2½ cups/100g kale

TO GARNISH

¼ cup/30g cashews

extra coconut yogurt

SWEET NAAN BREAD

½ cup/135ml unsweetened plant-based milk

½ teaspoon raw coconut nectar

1 teaspoon quick dried yeast

½ tablespoon chia seeds

¼ cup/40g brown rice flour

4 teaspoons/20g tapioca flour

1 teaspoon cornstarch/cornflour

1⅛ cups/135g buckwheat groats, plus extra for dusting

½ teaspoon baking powder

⅓ cup/40g golden raisins/sultanas

2 teaspoons nigella seeds

1 tablespoon coconut oil, plus extra for greasing, melted and at room temperature

2 tablespoons coconut yogurt

To make the naan bread, place the milk and coconut nectar in a small pan and gently heat until lukewarm. Add the yeast, stir or whisk well until dissolved, then remove from the heat and leave for 10 minutes.

Place the chia seeds in a small dish with 2½ tablespoons water, stir, and set aside for 10 minutes to swell.

Meanwhile, place the flours in a lightly oiled bowl with the cornstarch/cornflour, buckwheat, baking powder, golden raisins/sultanas, and nigella seeds. Add the milk mixture, oil, chia, and yogurt to the dry mix and combine well until a sticky dough is formed. Cover the bowl with a dish towel or plastic wrap and leave in a warm place for 1 hour to prove.

To make the daal, roughly chop the potatoes, carrots, and parsnips into ½ in/1cm chunks. Slice the onion and garlic. Heat the oil in a large saucepan, then add the onion and garlic with the fresh chili and spices. Allow the spices to infuse with the onion and garlic for a minute or so, then add the chopped vegetables and stir well to coat everything.

Rinse the lentils in cold water and add to the pan along with the stock. Cover with a lid and bring to the boil, then reduce the heat and simmer for 25–30 minutes or until the daal has a chunky but mushy consistency.

Around 10 minutes before the daal is ready, chop the kale, removing any tough stalks. Steam until lightly cooked either in a colander cover with a lid and set over a pan of boiling water or in an electric steamer.

Place the naan dough on a surface dusted with buckwheat and knead for a few minutes. Keep adding more buckwheat as you go to improve the handling and reduce the stickiness. Divide into four portions and flatten into oval shapes, then place on a nonstick baking sheet. Put the sheet under a preheated medium-high broiler/grill and cook for 10 minutes, turning halfway through, until golden brown.

Add the kale to the daal and stir well. Serve on warmed plates with a garnish of cashews, a spoonful of coconut yogurt, and the naan on the side.

Magical Mushrooms with Polenta

Ground yourself and boost your brain

Mushrooms are excellent for all-round health, especially during the dark winter months, because they contain high levels of vitamin D, which boosts mood, cognitive function, and the immune system. While the mushrooms in this recipe balance the root and brow chakras, the nutmeg and tarragon add a little stimulation to the latter, enhancing your perception and awareness. I have used some dried mushrooms here for the intensity of flavor.

Mix together the shiitake and wild mushrooms in a small bowl and cover with freshly boiled water. Set aside for 20 minutes.

Gently heat the olive oil in a saucepan and add the shallots, garlic, tarragon, and nutmeg. Sauté for about 5 minutes, until soft and tender.

Strain the soaked mushrooms, reserving the juice. Add the drained mushrooms to the pan with the fresh mushrooms and cook for 5 minutes over a medium heat, stirring well. Turn the heat down and stir in a tablespoon of the mushroom juice and the milk, then simmer gently for a further 5 minutes, adding salt and pepper to taste.

Now prepare the polenta. Place the milk and garlic in a pan and heat until almost at boiling point. Add the polenta in a steady stream, stirring well with a wooden spoon as you go. Bring to the boil and keep stirring until it reaches a smooth consistency (about 1–2 minutes). Add the olive oil and seasoning.

Serve on warmed plates with the magical mushrooms on top of the polenta.

CROWN
BROW
THROAT
HEART
SOLAR PLEXUS
SACRAL
ROOT

SERVES 4

MAGICAL MUSHROOMS

¾ cup/15g dried shiitake mushrooms

½ cup/10g dried wild mushrooms

2 tablespoons olive oil

3 shallots, finely chopped

2 garlic cloves, crushed

2 teaspoons dried tarragon

1 teaspoon ground nutmeg

1½ cups/100g sliced chestnut mushrooms

1½ cups/100g oyster mushrooms, sliced if large

¼ cup/50ml unsweetened plant-based milk

salt and freshly ground black pepper

POLENTA

1⅔ cups/400ml unsweetened plant-based milk

1 garlic clove, crushed

1 cup/175g gluten-free polenta

1 tablespoon olive oil

CROWN

BROW

THROAT

HEART

SOLAR PLEXUS

SACRAL

ROOT

SERVES 4

1 cup/185g dried adzuki beans, soaked overnight in cold water and drained

1 cup/180g dried black turtle beans, soaked overnight in cold water and drained

2 tablespoons cold-pressed canola/rapeseed oil

1 red onion, sliced

2 garlic cloves, sliced

1 red chili, finely chopped

1 green bell pepper, diced

1 yellow bell pepper, diced

1¾ cups/100g fresh shiitake mushrooms, sliced

1 teaspoon ground cinnamon

1 teaspoon cumin seeds

¼ teaspoon cayenne pepper

2 x 14 oz/400g cans of chopped tomatoes

bunch of cilantro/coriander, chopped

2 cups/320g brown basmati rice

sea salt and freshly ground black pepper

TO GARNISH

1 lime, cut into wedges

4 teaspoons chia seeds

2 avocados, chopped (optional)

Bean Feast Chili

Fire up your chakras

A traditional chili is one of those all-time classics that works very well as a wholesome vegan dish. I decided to use adzuki beans alongside the black beans as they are low in fat, full of protein and soluble fiber, and help to lower harmful LDL cholesterol. The dish works with all the chakras, but primarily the root and brow.

Rinse the soaked adzuki and black beans separately in fresh cold water. Place in separate pans of water and boil for 15 minutes, then cover and simmer for 30 minutes. Drain and set the beans aside.

Warm the oil in a large saucepan, add the onion and garlic, and sweat for 5 minutes. Add the chili to the pan, stir through, and sweat for a further 5 minutes. Add the peppers and mushrooms to the pan with the spices and stir thoroughly for 2–3 minutes over a medium heat. Add the tomatoes, beans, and cilantro/coriander. Simmer for 20 minutes, adding salt and pepper to taste.

Meanwhile, rinse the rice. Place in a medium-size pan with 4 cups/950ml water and a pinch of salt and cover with a lid. Bring to the boil, then simmer for 25 minutes until all the water has been absorbed.

Serve the rice and chili on warmed plates. Add lime wedges, scatter with the chia seeds, and serve with the chopped avocado on the side, if using. Also good with warm pita bread (see page 62).

CROWN

BROW

THROAT

HEART

SOLAR PLEXUS

SACRAL

ROOT

SERVES 4

SPECIAL EQUIPMENT

four ⅔ cup/150ml pudding bowls;
ice-cream maker

PUDDINGS

¼ cup/60ml canola/rapeseed oil, plus
extra for greasing

4 tablespoons ginger syrup (from a
jar of preserved/stem ginger)

1 tablespoon ground golden flaxseed

¼ cup/45g palmyra jaggery/SugaVida™

½ cup/80g brown rice flour

1½ teaspoons tapioca flour

1½ teaspoons baking powder

¼ teaspoon ground nutmeg

1 teaspoon ground ginger

4 pieces of preserved/stem ginger

⅓ cup/40g pecan halves, plus 4 for
the top

¼ cup/30g raw cacao nibs

ICE CREAM

14 oz/400g can of coconut milk

1¼ cups/300ml unsweetened plant-
based milk

½ cup/70g lacuma powder

¼ cup/75ml rice syrup

1 tablespoon ground star anise

Ginger and Pecan Puddings with Star Anise Ice Cream

Alternative Christmas indulgence

I've never been a fan of fruit-laden Christmas pudding, so decided to try something a little different. Lacuma is traditionally used to sweeten ice cream in its native Peru and contains essential trace elements potassium, sodium, calcium, magnesium, and phosphorus. In this recipe the brow receives stimulation from the star anise and ginger.

Lightly grease the pudding basins with rapeseed oil, then add 1 tablespoon of the stem ginger syrup from the jar into the base of each.

Mix the flaxseed with 3 tablespoons water. Mix the ¼ cup/ 60ml oil with the palmyra jaggery in a bowl, add the flaxseed mix and combine. Incorporate the flours, baking powder, nutmeg, ground ginger, and ⅓ cup/80ml water, mixing together until smooth. Chop the preserved/stem ginger into small pieces and add into the mix with the pecans and cacao nibs. Stir to mix thoroughly.

Spoon the mixture into the bowls (they should be about three-quarters full). Cover with plastic lids if you have them or parchment paper, pleated across the center, with a layer of foil over the top secured with string or an elastic band.

Place the covered bowls in two large pans and add water until to reach halfway up the bowls. Cover with tightly fitting lids, bring the water to the boil, then reduce the heat to simmering point and steam the puddings for 1–1¼ hours.

Meanwhile, make the ice cream by mixing all the ingredients in a bowl, then transfer to an ice-cream maker and churn for 40 minutes. Serve with the puddings and store the remaining ice cream in a sealed container in the freezer.

Note: If you don't have an ice-cream maker, place the mixed ingredients in a sealed container in the freezer for 3–4 hours, whisking every 30 minutes to prevent ice crystals forming.

CROWN

BROW

THROAT

HEART

SOLAR PLEXUS

SACRAL

ROOT

SERVES 8–10

SPECIAL EQUIPMENT
7 in/18cm nonstick springform cake pan

BASE

⅓ cup/30g raw cacao nibs

1¼ cups/125g walnut halves, plus extra to decorate

1½ tablespoons raw coconut oil, plus extra for greasing, melted and at room temperature

2 tablespoons rice syrup

3 teaspoons raw cacao powder

CAKE

3½ oz/100g raw dark vegan chocolate

1 teaspoon ground ginger

1 teaspoon ground cinnamon

¾ teaspoon freshly grated nutmeg

⅛ teaspoon cayenne pepper

1 cup/100g walnut halves

⅓ cup/100ml raw virgin coconut oil, melted and at room temperature

2 tablespoons raw cacao powder

pinch of sea salt

1¼ cups/250g unsweetened soya yogurt or coconut yogurt

Raw Spiced Chocolate and Walnut Cake

Awaken your psychic and cognitive abilities

This cake works primarily with the brow chakra to enhance intuition, psychic abilities, and cognitive function. The raw cacao and spices provide a stimulating kick to the chakra, but simultaneously the walnuts bring things back into balance so that you are not bouncing off the walls!

Lightly grease the cake pan with coconut oil.

To make the base, place all the ingredients in a food processor and mix until well combined and of a granola-type consistency—you are aiming for some texture and crunch. Spoon the mixture into the base of the cake pan, spreading and pushing down with the back of a spoon until firmly in place. Cover the pan with plastic wrap and place in the fridge.

To make the cake, break the chocolate into a small heatproof bowl. Bring a small amount of water to simmering point in the base of a small pan and place the bowl of chocolate over the pan, taking care that it does not to touch the water. Stir until melted, but do not overheat as this is a raw cake. Turn off the heat, add the ginger, cinnamon, nutmeg, and cayenne to the melted chocolate and stir to combine. Leave the bowl on top of the pan of water to keep the chocolate melted while you prepare the rest of the ingredients.

Finely grind the walnuts for the cake in a small blender and add to a food processor with the coconut oil, cacao powder, salt, and melted chocolate. Process well, then gradually add the yogurt and mix to a smooth consistency, being careful not to let it curdle.

Take the base out of the fridge and pour the cake mixture over the top, spreading it evenly using a spatula. Cover and place back in the fridge overnight. The next day, decorate the cake with walnut halves before serving. Keep the cake refrigerated and use within 4 days.

- CROWN
- BROW
- THROAT
- HEART
- **SOLAR PLEXUS**
- **SACRAL**
- ROOT

SERVES 8

SPECIAL EQUIPMENT
7 in/18cm nonstick springform
cake pan

3 tablespoons golden ground
flaxseed
¾ cup/180ml extra-virgin olive oil,
plus extra for greasing
½ cup/120ml rice syrup
2 cups/200g ground almonds
1 cup/175g polenta
3 teaspoons baking powder
2 tablespoons fresh thyme leaves,
plus extra sprigs to decorate
6 large mandarins
chopped almonds, to decorate

Mandarin and Thyme Polenta Cake

Boost your creativity and center of power

**During the winter months mandarins are so sweet
and tasty, and moist polenta cakes are such a great
way to enjoy gluten-free baking. The sacral and
solar plexus chakras are predominantly stimulated
in the recipe, with the hint of thyme activating the
heart and brow.**

Place the flaxseed in a bowl with ½ cup/135ml water and
leave to swell for 10 minutes.

Preheat the oven to 160°C fan/180°C/350°F/gas mark 3.
Lightly grease the cake pan with olive oil.

Mix the oil and three-quarters of the rice syrup together in
a large mixing bowl, then beat in the flaxseed mixture. Stir
in the ground almonds and fold in the polenta, baking
powder, and thyme. Add the zest and juice of four of the
mandarins and mix thoroughly. Add the remaining rice
syrup if the mixture is too dry.

Transfer the mixture to the cake pan. Peel and slice the two
remaining mandarins and carefully place the rounds on top
of the cake.

Place in the center of the preheated oven and bake for
1¼ hours. Remove the cake and cool on a wire rack.
Decorate the top with thyme sprigs and chopped almonds.

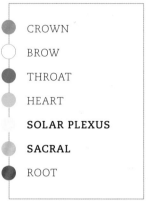

- CROWN
- BROW
- THROAT
- HEART
- **SOLAR PLEXUS**
- **SACRAL**
- ROOT

SERVES 10–12
(or less if you want more than one each!)

SNOW BALLS

1 tablespoon white chia seeds

1 cup plus 1 tablespoon/80g coconut flour

⅓ cup/30g dried shredded coconut

1½ tablespoons xylitol

¼ cup/60ml canned coconut milk

TO DECORATE

5 tablespoons filtered or mineral water

1½ tablespoons xylitol

3 tablespoons dried shredded coconut

Coconut Snow Balls

Little sweet bites

By amazing chance I forgot to use coconut oil in this recipe and it turned out just fine—what a bonus! The coconut milk provides enough fat content and, alongside the chia, helps to bind and moisten the cakes. These low GI cakes are suitable for diabetics and those on anti-candida diets, and work predominantly with the sacral and solar plexus chakras.

Place the chia seeds in a small bowl with 3 tablespoons water and leave to soak for 10 minutes.

Preheat the oven to 160°C fan/180°C/350°F/gas mark 4.

Mix the flour, shredded coconut, and xylitol together in a medium-size bowl. Gradually add the chia mixture and the coconut milk to the dry ingredients, mixing until it reaches a sticky consistency. If the mixture doesn't bind together, add a little more coconut milk.

Take a small amount of the mixture in your hand and roll into a ball 1¾ in/4cm in diameter (if the mixture is very sticky, it may help to dampen your hands), then place on a nonstick baking sheet, continuing until you have made 10–12 snowballs.

Place the baking sheet in the oven and bake the cakes for 15–20 minutes—you don't want them to go brown. Remove from the oven and cool on a wire rack.

Meanwhile, make a syrup for decoration. Place the water and xylitol in a small pan and bring to the boil, then reduce the heat and simmer for a minute. Leave to cool.

Take each cooled snow ball and brush a little of the syrup all over, then dip into shredded coconut. Leave for a few minutes to dry, then enjoy!.

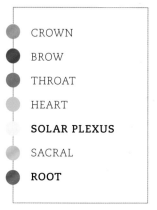

CROWN

BROW

THROAT

HEART

SOLAR PLEXUS

SACRAL

ROOT

English Muffins

A grounding and empowering classic

As a child, I loved eating toasted muffins in front of a roaring fire on a cold Sunday afternoon. It was our teatime ritual. This is a gluten-free, protein-based version of the English classic, made with calcium-loaded teff and amino acid-rich quinoa flours. The root and solar plexus chakras receive the most support here.

SERVES 4

1 teaspoon coconut palm sugar

⅔ cup/160ml warm water (approx 35°C/95°F)

1 tablespoon dried active yeast

½ cup/55g sorghum flour

⅓ cup/50g potato starch

½ cup/70g quinoa flour

¼ cup/40g teff flour

¼ cup/40g brown rice flour

1½ teaspoons baking powder

1 teaspoon xanthan gum

½ teaspoon sea salt

½ cup/120ml unsweetened plant-based milk

1 tablespoon ground golden flaxseed, mixed with 3 tablespoons water

2 tablespoons polenta

Mix the sugar and water in a small mixing bowl, sprinkle on the yeast, and whisk together thoroughly. Place somewhere warm (such as a slightly heated oven, turned off) for 10–15 minutes until the mixture has frothed up.

Mix all the dry ingredients together in a large bowl and set aside.

Add the milk and the ground flax mixture to the yeast, then combine thoroughly with the dry ingredients. Transfer the sticky dough into a large, lightly oiled bowl using a spatula, cover with plastic wrap or a dish towel, and leave in a warm place for 1¼ hours to prove.

Preheat the oven to 160°C fan/180°C/350°F/gas mark 4. Dust a baking sheet with half the polenta.

Coat your hands in flour and form the dough into four 3½ x 1¼ in/9 x 3cm circular muffins. Place on the polenta-covered baking sheet and pat the remaining polenta on top of each muffin. Bake in the center of the preheated oven for 35–40 minutes. Transfer to a wire rack to cool.

When ready to eat, slice in half and toast, then serve with vegan spread and the Christmas Jam on page 138.

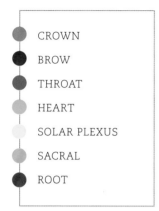

CROWN

BROW

THROAT

HEART

SOLAR PLEXUS

SACRAL

ROOT

Christmas Jam

Sweet comfort for all your chakras

In this recipe the fruits are barely cooked in order to preserve their nutrients. Low GI coconut palm sugar acts as the sweetener. The cranberries resonate with the root chakra, are full of phytonutrients, and are renowned for their support of the urinary and digestive tracts. Pears resonate with the heart chakra and can support cardiovascular health. Sea plant agar is a source of calcium, iron, and fiber, and helps to eliminate toxic waste from the body.

MAKES 6 x 8 oz/225g jars

4 mandarins

3 **tablespoons** agar flakes

6 pears

2½ **cups/250g** cranberries

1 **tablespoon** grated fresh ginger

zest and juice of 1 unwaxed lemon

1 **teaspoon** ground star anise

1 **teaspoon** ground cardamom

½ **teaspoon** ground nutmeg

1 **cup/140g** coconut palm sugar

½ **teaspoon** edible gold dust (optional)

First sterilize the jars by boiling the jars and their lids in a large pan of water for 10 minutes, then place in the oven on a low temperature to dry.

Juice the mandarins—you should end up with 1 cup/240ml juice. Place the juice in a medium-size pan with the agar and leave to stand for 10 minutes. Cover and bring the agar mixture to the boil momentarily, then reduce the heat and simmer for 5 minutes.

Chop the pears and place in a food processor with the cranberries, ginger, lemon zest and juice, and the spices. Process until combined. Add to the agar mixture with the sugar, bring to the boil, then simmer for 10 minutes, stirring occasionally.

Leave the jam to cool for 10 minutes, then stir through the edible gold dust, if using. Ladle into the jars, and seal the lids tightly. Label and give away as the perfect Christmas gift or serve with English Muffins (see page 136). Store for up to 3 weeks in the fridge.

Hot Chestnut Chocolate

Indulge all your chakras

Hot chocolate is a must in the winter months, and this thick and creamy raw cacao version is packed with low GI chestnuts and palmyra jaggery, which make it healthier than the more common sugar-laden Western versions of this drink.

CROWN
BROW
THROAT
HEART
SOLAR PLEXUS
SACRAL
ROOT

Preheat the oven to 200°C fan/220°C/425°F/gas mark 7.

Place the chestnuts on a baking sheet and roast in the preheated oven for 10–15 minutes. Remove from the oven and allow to cool for 5 minutes.

Shell the chestnuts, place in a mini food processor, and grind to a powder. Add the powder to a pan with the milk, whisk in the cacao and palmyra jaggery, then gently heat for a minute. Pour into a blender and blend for 1–2 minutes until thick and smooth in consistency. Return to the pan and heat gently, whisking in the spices.

Serve in large cups.

SERVES 2

SPECIAL EQUIPMENT
mini food processor or coffee grinder; blender

10 whole chestnuts (in shells)

1¾ cups/400ml unsweetened plant-based milk

2 tablespoons raw cacao

2 teaspoons palmyra jaggery/SugaVida™

½ teaspoon ground cardamom or cinnamon

pinch of cayenne pepper

Cranberry, Macadamia, and Cayenne Cookies

A lower chakra, energy-boosting treat

These cookies are moreish so beware! Macadamia nuts are renowned for their energy release and fiber content and are full of mono-unsaturated fatty acids, which can help to lower bad cholesterol and raise the good. The root, sacral, and solar plexus chakras are supported the most in this recipe.

CROWN

BROW

THROAT

HEART

SOLAR PLEXUS

SACRAL

ROOT

Preheat the oven to 170°C fan/190°C/375°F/gas mark 5.

In a bowl mix the oil with the palmyra jaggery and rice syrup. Add the flours, baking powder, cayenne, and milk and mix well to form sticky dough. Add the cranberries and macadamia nuts and knead them into the mixture using your hands.

Divide the dough into 8 balls. Place them on a nonstick baking sheet, and push them down to form cookies around 2½ in/ 6cm in diameter.

Place in the center of the preheated oven and bake for 15 minutes, then cool on a wire rack. For an indulgent treat, serve with Hot Chestnut Chocolate (see page 139).

MAKES 8

⅓ cup plus 1 tablespoon/100ml canola/rapeseed oil

¼ cup/45g palmyra jaggery/SugaVida™

3 tablespoons rice syrup

1½ cups/185g brown rice flour

2 tablespoons tapioca flour

1½ teaspoons baking powder

pinch of cayenne pepper

2 tablespoons unsweetened plant-based milk

¼ cup/30g dried cranberries

¼ cup/35g macadamia nuts

Index

Acknowledgments

I would like to thank Lauren Mulholland, Dawn Bates,
Cindy Richards, Sally Powell and all at CICO Books for their
assistance and support with this, my first publication. A
special thanks to Niels van Gjin for his beautiful design
work and patience. Much appreciation goes to my family
and friends for supporting me with unbounded love and
enthusiasm throughout the process. Thanks to my angels,
guides and departed loved ones, who are always with me,
and to Matthew for his encouragement, care and
assistance with the final edits.